TEAC LF

CW00503113

Computers
AND THEIR USE

SECOND EDITION

**Lionel Carter and
Eva Huzan**

Hodder & Stoughton

A MEMBER OF THE HODDER HEADLINE GROUP

British Library Cataloguing in Publication Data

ISBN 0 340 65494 5

First published 1984
Second edition 1996
Impression number 10 9 8 7 6 5 4 3 2 1
Year   1999 1998 1997 1996

Typeset by Transet Limited, Coventry, England.
Printed in Great Britain for Hodder & Stoughton Educational, a division of
Hodder Headline plc, 338 Euston Road, London NW1 3BH by Cox & Wyman Limited,
Reading, Berks.

CONTENTS

INTRODUCTION

This book is intended as an introduction to the wide variety of computer equipment and applications currently available.

Many computers, mainly microcomputers, are now used in offices, education and in the home. A very common use of computers in offices is for word processing. This provides an efficient means of preparing reports and standard letters which can be easily altered by making the changes on the computer's screen, and then storing the revised document on a disk file. Documents can be printed when required as 'perfect' copies.

The computer programs used for word processing, and other applications such as spreadsheets and graphics, are available 'off the shelf' as software packages. These have been written by professional programmers in software companies and are supplied with comprehensive documentation which often includes a tutorial or 'getting started' guide. Such business-type packages are also available for the school/college and home user. However, one of the most popular uses of home computers is for games, which use the computer's colour graphics and sound facilities.

Communicating with other people with common interests and sharing information is available to everybody with access to a microcomputer and the Internet. This gives people new possibilities to enhance their working lives and leisure activities through the millions of pages on the World Wide Web.

Some of the uses of computers are linked to social issues; benefits can be gained by using computers in health care and to help the disabled. However, because so much information is being stored in computers, great care must be taken to make sure that people not entitled to see the information cannot gain access to it. This involves using special techniques to prevent unauthorised access, and also legislation to control the setting up of data files and use of information contained in them.

Most commercial and industrial organisations find the use of computers essential in the running of their businesses and in the manufacture of their products. The vast amounts of information that have to be processed cannot be handled without computers. Robots are used in industry for automating processes which are repetitive, or those which need to be carried out in conditions unsuitable for people. The design of equipment can be aided by the use of computers, as can many of the manufacturing processes, and the planning and control of projects.

Today you are likely to come into contact with computers in your everyday life, for example when paying bills or using cash cards. These systems will have been designed by computer professionals. However, computing is no longer just the province of the specialist. You may want to use a computer yourself as a source of entertainment, for extending your knowledge, or for improving your business. This book has been written to help you to understand how computers can be used to achieve these aims. We start by explaining the factors to consider when choosing a personal computer.

Note: The term 'he' is used throughout this book for convenience only; it refers to both male and female computer users.

1

CHOOSING A
PERSONAL COMPUTER

Overview

Today there are many models of Personal Computers (PCs) on the market with different features and possible add-ons. This chapter discusses the aspects you should consider so that you can arrive at a computer configuration that meets your needs.

The first consideration is to decide on which applications you want to run on your PC. If you are a business user then you are likely to need, as a minimum, a spreadsheet package with graphics, a word processing package and, perhaps, presentation graphics. The use of these will be discussed in chapters 2, 3 and 4. If you are a home user, you will probably still need to use these packages but you will also need more facilities for playing computer games. For both types of user it is also important to have access to computers in the outside world.

This chapter is concerned with the equipment (hardware) and systems software that will allow you to run your applications software. By software we mean computer programs which comprise many instructions that are obeyed by the computer. Today, software is usually written in a computer 'language' such as BASIC or C.

Systems software is the essential part of your PC that turns the electronic and electro mechanical equipment (the hardware) into a usable computer. With new developments in this area, PCs are becoming very easy to use. Choosing a PC is made easier if you know something about the hardware and system software and how they work together to give you the computer environment that you require.

—— Processors and memory ——

Inside your computer there will be a number of computer chips containing many electronic circuits for processing information (processor chips) and for holding information during the processing (memory chips). These chips are called integrated circuits (see figure 1.1).

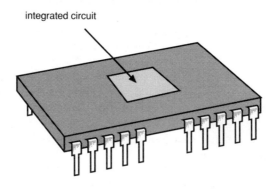

integrated circuit

Figure 1.1 A computer chip (integrated circuit)

The type of processor you choose will control the speed at which information is processed. The amount of memory also influences processing speed as a PC with more memory will need fewer transfers of instructions and data from the hard disk of your PC (see the next section).

You will find that the documentation supplied with your applications software will usually specify a minimum configuration and/or recommended configuration which will include the type of processor and the amount of memory required to run the application. If your PC does not have this configuration then you may find that the application will not run at all or will run too slowly for practical use.

It is possible to add extra memory chips at a later stage but it is not so easy, or may be impossible, to change the processor chip, although many innovative upgrade devices have appeared on the market. It is a good idea to get the fastest processor recommended and maximum amount of memory that you can afford as you will want to add further applications as you progress and as new applications come on the market. Also applications manufacturers (software companies) are continually improving their products and adding new features. Often this means that the programs become larger and may then require more memory and perhaps faster processors. Processors are generally quoted as being of a certain type and speed. The speed is given as a number of megahertz (MHz), although often just the number is quoted without the MHz.

Memory chips are available with different capacities, for example, your PC may have 8 megabytes (8 MB) of main memory known as RAM (Random Access Memory); this may be written to as well as read. It will often be made up of two 4 MB chips. You may be able to add more memory chips or replace the existing ones with higher capacity chips. There will be a maximum memory size stated for a particular model of PC. The minimum required for multimedia applications such as games may be 8 to 16 MB. Remember reference should be made to the recommended configurations for your applications for the type of processor, amount of memory and system environment.

Disk storage

There are basically three types of disk storage: 'floppy' disks, hard disks and CD ROM, which we will talk about later. 'Floppy' disks generally are 3.5" in diameter as standard and are no longer floppy but rigid. The term is historical from the time when computer disks were not rigid and the standard format was 5.25".

Your applications software is likely to be available on 3.5" disks or CD ROM. Such 3.5" disks are also useful for storing copies (back-ups) of your systems and applications programs and data. Generally, you are allowed to make one copy of programs that you have bought, for security reasons, and then you can store the master disks away safely. You should also take back-up copies of your data – this will be discussed in more details in chapter 5.

If you want to share information with a colleague 3.5" disks are also useful. For example, when we wrote this book we exchanged disks and then gave the final copy to our publishers in electronic format.

The same considerations apply in a business environment but there you are likely to have the added advantage of working on a network which makes sharing information much easier, more efficient and more controlled – this will be discussed in chapter 6.

Hard disks refer to large capacity disks which are the main means of permanent storage on your computer system. Whereas information stored in Random Access Memory is lost when the computer is switched off, the computer information on the hard disk stays there until deleted by the user.

For a self-contained, stand-alone PC, the minimum hard disk storage required will depend on how many system and applications programs and how much data you will need to have permanently available. It is time-consuming to load programs and data from 3.5″ disks so the capacity of the hard disk needs to be large enough to hold all this information with spare room for future expansion. You will also need some hard disk space during processing for intermediate and temporary files.

Hard disks come with varying capacity ranging from, say, 80 MB to several gigabytes (GB), where 1 GB is about 1000 MB (because of the way disks are constructed and computing quantities are measured it is, in fact, 1024 MB).

The hard disk may be internal, that is, inside the main box of the computer, together with the processor and memory boards, containing the computer chips and electronic circuits, or it may be separate, external, linked to the main box by a cable. The disk may be removable so that you can store a set of programs and data for some purpose on a hard disk and slot this in when required. This is also a way of making important information secure as the disk can be removed and locked away.

You should always back up your files as you create or work on them. In addition, because hard disks contain a large amount of information, it is very important to back up the hard disk on a regular basis. This can be done by copying the information on to floppy disks but as these have only a low capacity, you may need many disks to copy everything on your hard disk and this can be a tedious, time-consuming process.

An alternative is to use a tape drive which matches the capacity of your hard disk. This will allow you to back up the complete hard disk in one go and to restore the information in a similar way when required. Business users on a network are more likely to have back-ups of their hard disks made by their systems department using high capacity media such as DAT (digital audio tape) technology.

— Monitors and notebook computers —

Monitors or VDUs (visual display units) are available in different sizes and with different resolutions, the higher the resolution the sharper the screen image. For most applications you will need a standard colour monitor with good resolution. The resolution will be quoted as two numbers (X and Y) as X × Y. The figures refer to the number of dots or 'pixels' across and down the monitor screen, the more pixels the higher the resolution. Other options are larger screens, flat square screens, flicker-free and high-contrast screens.

Desktop computers have free standing monitors which can be put on top of the main box, on the desk or on a stand on the desk. Many people like to keep the main box off the desk for more desk space and put it on its side under the desk. Access to the on/off switch and floppy drive are essential so most models will have these at the front.

Another type of PC is the notebook computer which is a self-contained, light-weight machine, the size of a book. (see figure 1.2). The lid lifts up and contains the screen while the lower half of the box contains the processor, memory, floppy drive/CD ROM if fitted, hard disk, keyboard, a rechargeable battery and a 'mouse'. The latter may be integral, separate for use with a mouse mat, or clipped to the side. The mouse is used to move the pointer around the screen to select items – more about this later.

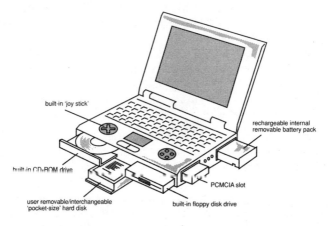

built-in 'joy stick'

rechargeable internal
removable battery pack

built-in CD-ROM drive

PCMCIA slot

user removable/interchangeable
'pocket-size' hard disk

built-in floppy disk drive

Figure 1.2 A notebook computer

The notebook screen may be colour or grey scale (different shades of grey) and may be of a variety of technologies. Lower resolution screens are of the LCD (liquid crystal display) or 'passive matrix' type and higher resolution screens are usually of the TFT or 'active matrix' type.

At the side of the machine, there may be one or two PCMCIA (Personal Computer Memory Card International Association) slots for 'credit card' size devices, such as fax/modems and network adapters for communications – discussed in chapter 6.

Notebook PCs are completely portable and can be used either on battery power or plugged into the mains. It is useful if the battery is charged while working with the notebook via the mains. To maintain the useful life of the battery, it needs to be recharged on a regular basis, and the PC's operating system (or the manual) should indicate when and how this needs to be done.

‎—— The windows environment ——

As we have mentioned, systems software turns the hardware into a usable computer. The most user-friendly environment is one based on the concept of windows and icons (small pictures of objects).

A windows environment will give the facility of dividing the screen into a number of windows which can overlap each other. Each window will contain a number of related icons, for example, you may have an applications window containing different icons, one for each type of application. Each icon should remind you of what the application does and also give the name of the application. Then when you want to run it, you would point to the icon by moving the pointer to it and click the mouse button (see the next section) to load the program into the PC's memory automatically.

The windows environment has revolutionised the way computers are used. However, because of the sophistication of these programs, more powerful processors and more memory is required than in the past. Fortunately the trend has always been for hardware to become less expensive for the same or greater power as the systems environment becomes more user-friendly. Thus the benefits of very easy-to-use computers are available to a wider and wider audience.

Pointing devices

The mouse is one type of pointing device which has a track ball that rolls over the desktop (using a mouse mat makes movement detection more positive). The computer detects the direction of mouse movement and moves the pointer or cursor across the screen appropriately. The pointer may be an arrow or highlighted square or some other symbol. For a particular application, each type of symbol will have a certain meaning.

Mouse devices are not the only type of pointers. The integral mouse on a notebook computer, for example, may be a roller ball fitted into the keyboard or a little toggle switch and there may be two keys representing the left and right-hand mouse buttons. A mouse may have one, two or three buttons, each of which has different functions and brings up different menus on the screen (lists of commands to select).

A single click of a mouse button usually has a different purpose to a double click. Software manufacturers tend to adopt the standard way of using a particular windows environment so that the general concept of using that environment with the mouse is the same for all applications. This means that once you have mastered the windows environment on your PC, you should easily be able to move to a different application without having to relearn how to move around the screen.

We have looked at the mouse pointing device which is very common for use with business-type applications. Other pointing devices include light pens and joysticks. Some applications involve the use of touch screens where your finger is the pointing device.

The screen of the computer is constantly being scanned at high speed by a beam of light. If a light sensitive pen is held against the screen, it registers a signal as the beam passes by. From a knowledge of the speed of the beam and the signal from the pen, the computer can calculate the position of the pen on the screen's surface. The touch screen works in a similar way but here your finger will be interrupting the beam to send a signal to the computer.

A joystick may be used for games which require the player to steer an object around the screen. Joysticks used with PCs are similar to those used with television games and usually allow movement along two axes (up/down, left/right), and there may also be a pushbutton as a 'fire' control. The simplest joysticks just 'switch on' the movement, say, upwards, when the joystick is moved in the up direction, and give no control over the speed of movement. The more elaborate joysticks have proportional controls, that is, the further the joystick is moved in any direction, the faster the object on the screen moves in that direction.

Printers

You will want to print out information produced on your PC whether this is a letter, report, graph, picture or a listing. The main considerations are concerned with the quality of the printout, speed of printing, the cost of the printer, the cost of supplies (paper, ribbons or, more usually, ink cartridges or toner, replacement parts), cost and type of maintenance available and compatibility with your applications. The latter is of utmost importance as incompatibility will result in you not being able to use certain printers at all. Generally, it is a matter of having the correct software, the printer driver, available for the particular model of computer and applications. For example, a word processing package will be supplied with a large variety of printer drivers and it is relatively easy to check if a particular printer model is on the list of drivers.

Nowadays, even low-cost printers can produce very good print quality. You will need to pay more if you require high quality and fast printing, a sheet feeder or colour in addition to mono (one colour, usually black on white, or other coloured paper) printing. The quality is quoted as for screen resolution as the number of dots across (X) and down (Y) of an area on the paper (X × Y); the greater the number of dots the higher the resolution and quality. Quality also depends on the printer technology used and is best judged by looking at samples.

You may have special requirements as to size of paper, use of labels and acetate sheets (for presentations), multipart stationery, specific fonts (print size or style), all of which are available if you choose the right printer. Remember this must also be compatible with your environment, systems and applications software.

Other considerations are the length of the warranty and type of maintenance, for example, on-site or return to supplier/manufacturer, a factor to be considered for any part of your computer system including the PC itself. If any part of the system needs to be returned for repair, there will be a delay before it comes back to you and a replacement may be required so that you can carry on using the equipment.

In a business environment, you may be given access to a variety of shared printers across a network. Your printer set up will need to be such that you can send your work for printing by selecting the appropriate network printer from your PC. Your printout will then go into a queue for that printer and be printed out when it gets to the top of the queue.

Network printers allow users to share access to more sophisticated facilities. The printers may be set up to contain special paper in different trays; for example, a printer may have three trays for A4 paper, letter-headed stationery and labels. Network printers may be company wide or local to a department so that you can easily collect your printouts or use the manual feed option when requiring special paper.

Multimedia

Many computer games, teaching materials and some business applications require the use of sound, still and moving pictures (video). These facilities are termed multimedia and these types of application require special hardware and software for your PC.

Your PC may already incorporate a sound card (circuit board with sound hardware) and compatible sound software and a speaker. If not, it should be possible, depending on your PC model, to add these on. Generally, an inbuilt speaker will not be of high quality and a pair of stereo speakers may need to be added. The type of sound card required will also vary according to the type of application, higher quality being required for music compared to sounds for games.

Standards are available for pictures and video clips available from libraries of these on disk, but may require additional video software.

The multimedia software may be provided on 3.5" disks or on CD ROM. The compact disks used with CD ROM hardware have a different format from the conventional music CDs. ('ROM' stands for 'read only memory', i.e. you cannot write to it or change it.) An advantage for both the software manufacturer and the user is that CDs have a much higher capacity so that an applications program which runs over many 3.5" disks can fit on to one CD ROM. This saving in cost may be passed on to the user so that the same software on CD ROM may be less expensive than on 3.5" disk, and in many cases will not be available other than on CD ROM.

CD ROMs are also used to provide fast access to large amounts of information, such as encylopaedias and for training materials. Many computer magazines, which incidentally are an excellent source of up-to-date information, give away free CD ROMs containing programs, including games and various software routines, for readers to try out on their PCs.

CD ROMs are written to by the software manufacturers; the PC user cannot record information on these without extra, expensive hardware. However, if you have sound and video facilities and the appropriate programs on your PC to manipulate these, then you can create your own multimedia effects and store these on your hard disk.

Add-ons

So far we have discussed the hardware/software required for the most common PC applications that you are likely to use in the home or business environments. There are many more ways that you can use your PC and for these you may require extra equipment and software. We will consider just some of these in this section.

When you want to connect to computers in the outside world over the telephone line, you will need to have a modem. This can be a box which is external to your computer and linked by a cable to it or it can be a card or board within your computer. What the modem does very simply is to convert the electronic (digital) signals to and from the computer into audio signals.

The process of converting from digital into audio signals is called modulation and the process of converting from audio into digital signals is called demodulation. A modem (modulator-demodulator) needs to be connected between the computer and an ordinary telephone line to perform this task. A lead from the modem plugs into your telephone socket to make the necessary connection.

It is more useful to have a fax/modem card as this enables you to send faxes, that you have created, say, with a word processing package, and to receive faxes from the outside world which can be viewed and stored on your computer, and printed when required. You will need special fax software – this will be discussed in chapter 6.

Another useful device is a scanner which can be hand-held (see figure 1.3), mobile or sheet-feed. The scanner can scan colour or grey scale images (typically 16.8 million colours or 256 shades of grey) from pictures and documents straight into your PC.

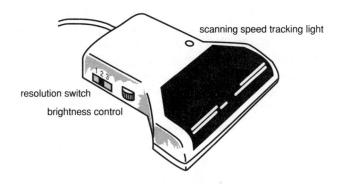

scanning speed tracking light

resolution switch

brightness control

Figure 1.3 A hand-held scanner

Most PCs have at least one parallel printer port and the scanner can be plugged into this. The picture/document is fed into the scanner (or the scanner is passed over these) and will appear on the screen for viewing and editing/enhancing with the software supplied with the scanner. Some scanners also double up as fax and copier machines.

Another PC add-on is the bar code reader. Bar codes are used on many items bought in shops to encode information about that particular item. These codes appear as a collection of thin and thick black lines separated by spaces. When a light sensitive pen is passed along the bar code, the pattern of light which it reflects passes to a sensor in the head of the light pen and can be decoded by the bar code reader unit which is connected to the PC by a cable. A magnetic strip is a similar idea but the code is recorded on a short narrow strip of magnetic material, which may be incorporated as part of a label. When the item is sold, a wand (hand-held pen) is passed over the ticket and all the details are recorded on the PC. The two methods are useful in shops, at conference/exhibitions and the like, because they are quicker and more accurate than having to enter the data by hand at a keyboard.

Summary

This chapter has introduced you to the concepts and aspects that you need to consider when choosing a PC. There are many technical considerations which we have covered in outline. Some of the equipment and software will be discussed further in the applications chapters. For a more detailed description and explanation of the technical issues involved in choosing a PC, we would like to refer you to *Teach Yourself Choosing a PC* by Alan Clark.

2

SPREADSHEET AND GRAPHICS

────── What is a spreadsheet? ──────

Electronic spreadsheet packages allow you to build up a worksheet on your computer screen. The particular advantage of these packages is that, once built up, any numeric changes made to the worksheet immediately cause the computer to recalculate any dependent values. As the spreadsheet can be built up by the user and printouts obtained without any computer programming knowledge, these packages are powerful tools for 'what if' investigations.

The spreadsheet is initially presented to you as a blank 'sheet' consisting of many rows and columns, for example, 256 vertical columns and 16,384 horizontal rows, giving a total of over 4 million cells. Each cell is defined by its column letter, A through to Z, then AA through to AZ, etc., and row number 1 through to 16,384, in the package that we are using. The computer screen provides a 'window' on the worksheet, which you can move to view any part.

There are basically three types of entry that the user can make on the worksheet after positioning the screen cursor over the required part of the worksheet to highlight it. An item of text, heading, label, and so on, can be entered simply by typing it in. Similarly, numeric values can be typed in directly from the keyboard. The third type of entry is a formula. A formula is entered by specifying the appropriate coordinates (column and row identifiers) of the required cells on the worksheet, having previously positioned the cursor over the cell where the formula is to be implemented. You may need to enter a symbol to indicate that you are using a formula, for example, an equals sign (=):

=A6+D7

may be entered when the cursor is over E8. The result of adding the value currently in A6 (column A, row 6) to that in D7, will then be displayed in E8. Subsequently, changing the value in A6 and/or D7 will cause the result in E8 to be recalculated immediately and displayed in E8. As well as the plus sign (+), we can use a minus sign (–), an asterisk (*) for multiplication and a forward slash (/) for division. We can also use brackets in our formula. The rules usually are that the parts of the formula in brackets are worked out first by the computer, then division and multiplication, followed by addition and subtraction.

A simple example

The principles of using a spreadsheet will be illustrated by a simple but realistic example: we will consider the hiring of a hall from, say, a sports club, whose aim is to make a profit to buy equipment and enhance facilities for its members. The voluntary, unpaid, committee meets at six-monthly intervals to consider how well the hall hire business has been going in the preceding six months. It is the job of the honorary treasurer to prepare a spreadsheet to give details of the income and expenditure and to present this and associated graphs to the committee for approval, discussion and forward planning.

The EXPENDITURE spreadsheet will show every item of expenditure by name. Some items will comprise regular payments, for example, the monthly payments to the caretaker which will appear six times on the six-monthly speadsheet, whereas the council rates will only appear once as these are paid every six months in our example. Some items will be one-offs, such as replacing a broken window pane, or will be bought when required, for example, electric light bulbs.

Building up the spreadsheet

Let us see how the treasurer would build up his spreadsheet. We will keep the design simple, keeping in mind that we can enhance the appearance of the spreadsheet later once all the information has been entered.

The first six-monthly period runs from April to September. We will put the date in column A, details in words in column B, and head the remaining columns as Rates, Maintenance, Caretaker, Lighting, Consumables and Insurance. Each of these columns will contain the actual amounts spent on the different items and we will want to add these up as row totals and column totals so as to arrive at a grand total for the six-month period.

To start with all the columns will be the same width, by default. We will change that to have wider or narrower columns as required. For example, the details column containing the item description will need to be wider than the columns containing the numbers. We can alter the width at any time by clicking on Format, Columns, Width, from the 'pull-down' menus, and finally putting a number in for the column width.

We could instead type the headings in first and then change the column width to suit. You do not lose the characters typed in if the width is too narrow; usually, they just do not show on the screen until you widen the column. If a cell contains a number that is too large for the width, it may show asterisks until you widen it to allow for the largest number in that column.

Text can be justified left or right or centrally in a column, so we will place our column headings centrally and left justify the item details in column B. The numbers are all in pounds sterling with two decimal places for the pence so we will choose this format for the appropriate cells. Once the headings and dates for the regular payments are put in, we can enter the numbers. The caretaker's monthly fee is the same for each of the six months so we will enter this only once and then copy it to the other cells as appropriate.

The treasurer would add the other items to the spreadsheet as the payments were allocated. The totals will be created using a SUM function, and this will be adjusted when more items and numbers are entered.

The spreadsheet at the end of the six month period is shown in figure 2.1. This can be enhanced by including lines, different fonts and emboldening, and printed out without the column (letter) and row (number) identifiers.

EXPENDITURE for Year xxxx – 4th April to 3rd October

	A	B	C	D	E	F	G	H	I
1	Date	Details	Rates	Maintenance	Caretaker	Lighting	Consumables	Insurance	TOTAL
2									
3	08-Apr	Council rates	£253.75						£253.75
4	23-Apr	Monthly fee			£80.00				£80.00
5	04-May	Contents						£256.45	£256.45
6	12-May	Lighting				£260.78			£260.78
7	23-May	Monthly fee			£80.00				£80.00
8	17-Jun	Paint windows		£140.34					£140.34
9	23-Jun	Monthly fee			£80.00				£80.00
10	07-Jul	Replace pane		£10.67					£10.67
11	14-Jul	Indemnity						£563.62	£563.62
12	19-Jul	Cleaning materials					£36.75		£36.75
13	23-Jul	Monthly fee			£80.00				£80.00
14	12-Aug	Lighting				£176.56			£176.56
15	23-Aug	Monthly fee			£80.00				£80.00
16	29-Aug	Sundries					£20.64		£20.64
17	02-Sep	Electric bulbs					£6.89		£6.89
18	07-Sep	Leak in kitchen		£36.84					£36.84
19	23-Sep	Montly fee			£80.00				£80.00
20									
21		TOTAL	£253.75	£187.85	£480.00	£437.34	£64.28	£820.07	£2,243.29

Figure 2.1 Expenditure spreadsheet with cell identifiers

Functions

The INCOME spreadsheet will be on a monthly basis and we will be consolidating this into a six-monthly summary at the end of the period together with the six-monthly expenditure summary.

We will need to use further formulae and functions for the INCOME spreadsheet. For example, the hall fee may depend on whether it is required for a morning, afternoon or evening session at £20 per session, or any combination of these, whether it is on a regular basis, when a discount may apply, and whether more setting up or cleaning is required (as for the craft fair). We can put the basis for this costing to the side of the actual spreadsheet to enable us to build up the actual costs as a formula.

For example, the barn dance group meets weekly and pays in advance so are entitled to a 10% discount on the hall fee (not on the use of the kitchen), hence our formula is =20*4*0.9. The craft fair is for the whole day but needs setting up the evening before and clearing up the morning after (£10 × 2) when extra help is required from the caretaker charged at £5 an hour for six hours.

Other groups, such as the photographic society and local history group, also meet on a regular basis, four times and twice per month, respectively. As these are billed for each occasion they only qualify for a 8% and 4% discount. We can build our rules into the spreadsheet and apply them as required. The final INCOME spreadsheet for April is shown in figure 2.2. Notice that we have enhanced the appearance of this by using different fonts and emboldening. It is best not to overdo this and make the spreadsheet 'too pretty'; the aim is to achieve a professional appearance for good communication of information.

INCOME for the month of APRIL xxxx					
Date	Details	Hall fee	Use of kitchen/staff	Hire equipment	TOTAL
06-Apr	Bridge Tournament	£20.00	£10.00		**£30.00**
07-Apr	Barn Dance/for month	£72.00	£10.00	£45.00	**£127.00**
08-Apr	Photo Society	£18.40	£10.00	£15.00	**£43.40**
10-Apr	Local History Group	£19.20	£10.00	£15.00	**£44.20**
14-Apr	Craft Fair	£100.00	£50.00		**£150.00**
15-Apr	Photo Society	£18.40	£10.00	£15.00	**£43.40**
16-Apr	Community Action grp	£20.00			**£20.00**
20-Apr	Jumble Sale	£20.00	£10.00		**£30.00**
22-Apr	Photo Society	£18.40	£10.00	£15.00	**£43.40**
24-Apr	Local History Group	£19.20	£10.00	£15.00	**£44.20**
29-Apr	Photo Society	£18.40	£10.00	£15.00	**£43.40**
	TOTAL	**£344.00**	**£140.00**	**£135.00**	**£619.00**

Figure 2.2 Income spreadsheet for April (hall hire example)

The following month we can take a copy of the April spreadsheet, delete any items not paid for that month and add new items.

Updating spreadsheets

At the end of the six-month period, the treasurer will be ready to summarise or consolidate income and expenditure on one spreadsheet. Similarly, at the end of the year, all the information for the year can be summarised in one spreadsheet as show in figure 2.3.

INCOME & EXPENDITURE SUMMARY for year ending xxxx									
INCOME									
Month	**Hall fee**	**Use of kitchen/staff**	**Hire of equipment**	**TOTAL**					
Apr	£344.00	£140.00	£135.00	**£619.00**					
May	£400.00	£130.00	£105.00	**£635.00**					
Jun	£320.00	£120.00	£150.00	**£590.00**					
Jul	£360.00	£110.00	£105.00	**£575.00**					
Aug	£260.00	£100.00	£90.00	**£450.00**					
Sep	£280.00	£110.00	£120.00	**£510.00**					
Oct	£340.00	£90.00	£90.00	**£520.00**					
Nov	£260.00	£100.00	£105.00	**£465.00**					
Dec	£400.00	£140.00	£105.00	**£645.00**					
Jan	£300.00	£100.00	£75.00	**£475.00**					
Feb	£220.00	£70.00	£120.00	**£410.00**					
Mar	£280.00	£110.00	£105.00	**£495.00**					
TOTAL	**£3,764.00**	**£1,320.00**	**£1,305.00**	**£6,389.00**					
EXPENDITURE									
6 Month Periods		**Rates**	**Maintenance**	**Caretaker**	**Lighting**	**Consumables**	**Insurance**	**TOTAL**	
04-Apr	03-Oct	£253.75	£187.85	£480.00	£437.34	£64.28	£820.07	**£2,243.29**	
04-Oct	03-Apr	£253.75	£97.67	£480.00	£367.25	£89.53	£0.00	**£1,288.20**	
	TOTAL	**£507.50**	**£285.52**	**£960.00**	**£804.59**	**£153.81**	**£820.07**	**£3,531.49**	

Figure 2.3 Income and expenditure for year

The information for each month is extracted from the monthly INCOME spreadsheet taking the totals for each of the income columns and creating a grand total for the six months or year. The EXPENDITURE part of the spreadsheet is shown as the totals for each of the two six-month periods.

We are now ready to turn the spreadsheet summary into a graph showing the profit or loss.

Graphs

Most spreadsheets have a large variety of graph types to choose from. Data from the worksheet cells is shown as bars, lines, pie slices, etc. Within each type of chart, you may be given a choice of subtypes. For example, a bar chart may show the different columns representing the different types of income for each of the 12 months side by side. Alternatively, we could use a stacked bar chart where the columns for each month show the items one on top of each other.

In each case, the items would be in different columns, in different shades of grey (or in different colours) and/or patterned to distinguish them. A legend would show the colour representation for each item type, as shown in figure 2.4 of the income bar chart for the year.

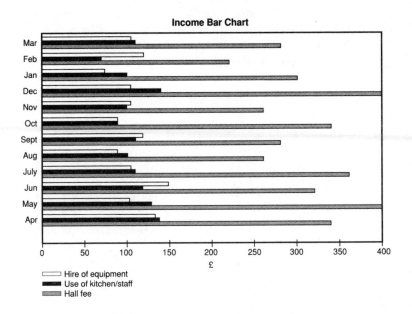

Figure 2.4 Income bar chart

The chart could also be shown three-dimensionally or a pie-chart could be created with the same data. It may be appropriate to display the data with more than one type of chart on the same graph, for example, a bar chart and a line graph.

There are facilities for enhancing the graph to improve the titling and labelling. The aim should be to show the information in a clear way so that the recipient of the chart can understand the meaning easily.

—— Drawing and enhancing ——

You may want to present your speadsheets and graphs in a report, as we will do in the next chapter, or incorporate them in you presentation (chapter 4 will discuss this).

As far as the chart of income and expenditure is concerned, the treasurer will want to show the details of these side by side, perhaps as stacked columns. Also, as the aim of the sports club is to make a profit, this needs emphasising, which we can do by drawing in the profit section as shown in figure 2.5, using a broken line and double-headed arrow selected from the drawing tools. Also we have put a shadow on the profit box to highlight it. This will show the committee at a glance all the details it needs to know whether as part of the treasurer's report or in his presentation. Again simplicity should be the keynote.

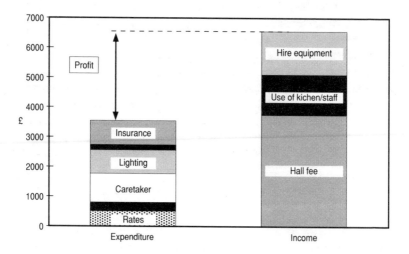

Figure 2.5 Chart showing profit

3

WORD PROCESSING AND DESKTOP PUBLISHING

The typing revolution

Typed documents are required for many purposes such as letters, reports, newsletters and legal papers. Invariably mistakes are made by the person typing and need to be corrected. Before the advent of word processors, there were a number of different methods for correcting documents to achieve a final perfect version, such as using correcting fluid. This was not always a satisfactory solution, particularly for legal documents which often had to be retyped several times because alterations are not acceptable.

The use of word processors (WPs) completely revolutionised the way documents are produced. Early word processors were often dedicated computers with specialised software for editing, reformatting and printing text. Word processing programs were also available for use on PCs but tended to have fewer facilities. Today the word processing software available as part of complete office suites of programs for PCs (including spreadsheets, graphics, presentation graphics and databases), is very sophisticated and rich in features making the dedicated wordprocessor machines redundant.

Many people in offices and in the home now use word processing packages to produce high quality documents. These have also largely replaced specialised desktop publishing systems as camera ready copy for printers can easily be produced with WP software or the information can just be passed on in electronic form (on disk) for the printers who then use computers attached to their printing equipment for formatting the text and inserting pictures.

Once you have used a WP package you will never want to go back to the typewriter, even though some electronic typewriters also have WP features. One of the main advantages of using WP software on your PC is that you can integrate the text with information output from other software packages, for example, to insert a graph or picture into your report, and this will give you maximum flexibility in the production of your documents.

—— Word processing features ——

There are some essential features that all WP packages should have. First, you must be able to type your text in as quickly as you can without having to press a key to go to the next line. The software should automatically wrap-around, taking a complete word to the next line if necessary, so that you only press the Return key when you get to the end of a paragraph or want to put in another line. (Some keyboards have the word 'Enter', or a hooked arrow on the Return key.)

You should be able to set the margins on the left and right-hand sides of the pages, also top and bottom, to a specific number of centimetres (with decimal places) as required for the particular document that you are working on. There should be a choice of justification of the text. For example, if the text is to be right-justified then, as well as word-wrapping, the software will spread words out on the line so that they all line up on the right-hand side of the page.

A ruler line will give the tab and margin settings and one or more status lines will show the current cursor (e.g. flashing square or line) position as a line and column number, and the file reference.

As you type in the text, you should be able to insert, change or delete characters, words or whole sections, and also move these to different positions in the text. Usually, to insert something you position the cursor at the insertion point and type in the text. To change something, you highlight it and type the change and to delete something you highlight the section to be deleted and then press the back space or delete keys.

Having typed the text in, you should be able to apply different styles to different parts of the document. You may want various levels of headings, some with bigger fonts (point sizes) and different types of font, as selected from a list of choices. Some typing may need to be bold and/or italic. You should be able to set the spacing between paragraphs and between the headings and the following text.

You may want different indentations, automatic numbering and bullet points, where each point in a list has a symbol in front of it, perhaps a solid circle or square. You should be able to set tabs for each style so that by pressing the tab key the cursor will jump to a particular position on the line. Several tab positions may be set up for each style. The style you have set up will be stored with the document.

An example

Figure 3.1 shows a simple example of formatting text. The programme for a school concert uses different types and sizes of fonts, with some text in bold and/or italic. The text was first typed in and

MOZART CONCERT

to be given by

THE NEW TOWN SCHOOL ORCHESTRA

at 7pm on Wednesday 5th March at the school

Peter Johnson *conductor* and **Helen Smith** *piano*

PROGRAMME

- **Piano Concerto No 21**

- **Marriage of Figaro Overture**

- **Symphony No 40**

- **Eine kleine Nachtmusik**

Please make a donation to the school fund when booking your ticket with the School Secretary

Figure 3.1 School concert programme

then selected by highlighting particular sections. The styling was applied to each section in turn as required. For example, the main heading was centred, emboldened and given a large-size font. The works in the programme were made into a bulleted list and indented.

——— Organising your files ———

It is a good idea to save your work often in a file as you proceed so as not to lose this if there is a power failure or your computer goes down for any reason. Your intermediate and final drafts will thus be stored safely on your hard disk.

In a business environment, where you may be working on a network, you may be required to file your work in certain directories that have been set up by your department or the systems people. When you are filing your work on a stand alone computer you need to be just as organised so that you can retrieve your work easily and quickly.

Basically, you want to have a hierarchical structure for your files. By that we mean that you will have a main directory divided into subdirectories, which may be divided into further subdirectories until there is an appropriate place for that particular file. This will enable you to locate the file easily without having to keep a note of where it is filed. In addition, you may want to print the location of the file in the document's footer, say, the left bottom corner, but this may not always be appropriate.

Let us consider that you want to file your correspondence under different headings. One possible file structure could be as shown in figure 3.2. We can see how part of this would look in a computer directory on the c: drive (the hard disk) as follows:

    c:\letters\utils\electric

where 'utils' is a subdirectory of letters and 'electric' is a subdirectory of utils. Notice that a maximum of eight characters (letters, numbers and the underline) are allowed for naming computer directories.

When we want to file a letter to the electricity company, we would select the electricity directory and perhaps name the file by its date, say l_xx0624.doc (letter dated 24th June in year xx), so that all our letters to the electricity company would be stored together.

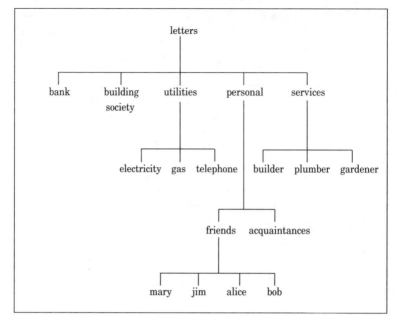

Figure 3.2 Hierarchical file structure for letter storage

There are no hard and fast rules so you will need to create the directory structures that will help you to retrieve your files easily.

Templates

It can take some time to set up appropriate styles for a document and although these are stored with the document you may want to create a number of documents with the same styles. In a business environment, it is likely that the company will want everyone to produce letters, faxes, reports, proposals, quotations, etc. in the same style so that there is consistency. This may be achieved by the use of templates.

A template will specify the different styles that are available for headings, normal text, normal indentation, numeric indentation, prices, headers, footers, etc., and perhaps standard text to be inserted in the document, for example, for a letter or a fax. As well as giving consistency, using templates also saves users a considerable amount of time.

Instead of having to set the styles each time, you select the appropriate template and then as you type the text you select the style by its name from a list.

We will look at an example of a report to illustrate the use of templates (figure 3.3). First of all 'New' is selected from the file menu, then the report template and heading 1 are selected. Heading 1 is the main heading style. When the main heading is typed, it will automatically be in the heading 1 style, that is, in Arial font, point size 16 and bold. Heading 2 is a subheading of heading 1 and is in Arial, 14, bold and italic. Heading 3 is a subheading of heading 2 and is in Times New Roman font, point size 13, bold and italic. Normal text is in Times New Roman, point size 12, and we would probably also have normal or numeric indentation styles in the template as a minimum. (Note that the illustration is not to scale but shows the relative sizes of the headings.)

Craft Fair – April xxxx

Summaries from Stall Holders

1. Watercolour Paintings

This year we found that the flower and animal paintings were the most popular. Sets of small framed paintings sold particularly well.

2. Homemade Produce

Everything was sold although we had to make some reductions towards the end. As usual, jams, chutneys and small cakes went very quickly and we could have sold more of these.

3. Dried flowers

Our sales were somewhat disappointing this time compared to our fair in November although we had a lot of visitors to our stall. From their comments it would appear that prices were higher than expected and there was less demand for making the flowers up into displays for presents.

Figure 3.3 Example of using a report template

You can either choose the style before you type the text or choose the text and then apply the style. You can change the style of any section at any time by highlighting it and applying a new style. Also, although you are using a template, you can still modify the style and apply it to different parts of the document if this is required.

New templates are often created by modifying existing templates which is usually easier than creating a template from scratch. Most WP software will have some standard templates as part of the package.

——— Bringing in other work ———

The WP package may have graphical and drawing facilities with it. Alternatively, you may want to bring in graphs and pictures from

Our expenditure for the first six months of the year is shown in the table below.

	Rates	Maintenance	Caretaker	Lighting	Consumables	Insurance
April	£253.75	£0.00	£80.00	£0.00	£0.00	£0.00
May	£0.00	£0.00	£80.00	£260.78	£0.00	£256.45
June	£0.00	£140.34	£80.00	£0.00	£0.00	£0.00
July	£0.00	£10.67	£80.00	£0.00	£36.75	£563.62
August	£0.00	£0.00	£80.00	£176.56	£20.64	£0.00
September	£0.00	£36.84	£80.00	£0.00	£6.89	£0.00
Total	£253.75	£187.85	£480.00	£437.34	£64.28	£820.07

The following points should be noted:

1. Some maintenance was required and a figure for this should be included in future budgets. It is suggested that £1,000 would be appropriate.

2. The figure for consumables was modest and below our estimate of £300 per annum.

3. It may be possible to get a reduction in the insurance premium by obtaining competitive quotations.

Figure 3.4 Part of management report with spreadsheet

other sources. In a report on the hire of the sports club hall, as given in the example in chapter 2, we would bring in the spreadsheets and /or graph created with the spreadsheet software. This is illustrated in figure 3.4 which shows part of the management report on the hall hire example given in chapter 2.

A spreadsheet of a summary of the costs per month has been imported and automatically converted into a table in the word processing document. It was then reformatted using one of the supplied standard formats.

There may be a library of pictures supplied with your WP package containing a number of different individual pictures, called clip art, which can be brought into your document. Figure 3.5 shows an invitation to a party with clip art added.

You are invited to a

FANCY DRESS PARTY

at

150 New Road, Old Town

on

Saturday, 23rd September

starting at 2.30 pm

<u>PRIZES WILL BE AWARDED</u>

Please bring something to eat and drink

RSVP

Figure 3.5 Party invitation with clip art

Advanced facilities

So far we have described a range of fairly standard uses of WP software. This section covers additional, more advanced facilities, available with some word processing packages:

- newspaper style columns
- tables and frames
- forms
- mail merge
- macros.

Newspaper style columns

A brochure for our hire hall example may require the use of newspaper style columns. Rather than having the text go right across the page, we may want to have two or more columns. By choosing a newspaper style for the columns, the text will flow from the bottom of one column to the top of the next. We may also want to add a vertical line between the columns.

Tables and frames

It is useful to be able to create tables for columns of figures or for putting text next to a graph or picture. Such a feature avoids having to use tabs for spacing out the information. Also, the table can be put in a frame and moved around the document as a complete unit until the final position has been selected.

Forms

In a business environment, it is useful to have a forms facility. Types of forms that can be used on-line through a network by different users include fax forms, request forms, order forms, expense forms, etc. These forms are set up by creating a new template for each type of form and inserting grids using the tables facility, typing in text and adding various form fields. If you are not familiar with databases, chapter 7 explains the various terms such as fields.

The users can then select the required form from a list, type in the variable information and print it. Names and addresses and other information may be inserted automatically from databases; this facility is called mail merge and is dealt with in the next section. A protection facility will prevent the users changing the form as they fill it in.

Mail merge

As with every computer application, the possibility of exploiting the fact that the information already exists in electronic format should be explored. You should never have to type information into the computer more than once but be able to extract it and use it in different applications. The mail merge facility allows you to do this.

Merge fields are put into the main document which refer to fields on the actual database. When the document is merged, the merge fields are replaced with the actual information on the database.

You may just be pulling off a company name, address and contact for one letter or for a number of personalised letters for a mailshot. Once the information is on the database, selections can be made according to search criteria, for example, mailing people or companies who have certain attributes. The mail merge facility saves users a great deal of time and is more accurate than typing in the information again.

Macros

Another facility that advanced users of WP software may use is a macro. A macro is a series of commands, in this case WP commands, which can be run by just selecting the macro. One common way of creating a macro is to record the series of commands, with a record facility, and then giving the macro a name, adding it to a menu, or as an icon. When you want to run the macro, you only need to select it and all the commands will be run as though you were selecting them one at a time.

4

PRESENTATION GRAPHICS

— The use of presentation graphics —

Presentation graphics software allows you to create slides, which can contain text, graphics and pictures, easily and quickly. Before such software was available, it was often necessary to employ specialists to achieve a professional look. Today, the best presentation graphics software incorporates templates, designed by professional artists, which you can use as they stand or modify to your own design.

You can build up your presentation in outline, create the slides, reorganise the order in which they will be presented, add graphs and pictures, produce handouts for your audience and notes for your talk.

You may be giving a presentation to a small group with limited technical resources, perhaps just using an overhead projector. In this case, you can output the slides onto acetate film. For a larger group or for a regular presentation, you may want to have 35 mm slides created.

There are many different ways of presenting your slides. One of the most flexible ways is to output the slides from your computer when this is plugged into the presentation equipment. The various methods are covered in the last section of this chapter.

—— Design considerations ——

The main design consideration is the clear presentation of your ideas.

This means keeping the messages simple and not putting too much information on a single slide.

The slide show should appear interesting and focus the audience's attention on the different points that you will be explaining. The titles should be in a larger font to the rest of the text and perhaps in a different type of font. Pictures may be included where appropriate but should not be overdone. Some slides may benefit from the inclusion of a picture while others may be better without.

Colour can have a useful impact but again overdoing this should be avoided by limiting the number of colours used. When you are building up a series of bullet points, it may be useful to change colour as a new one is brought in. It is also effective to bring the bullet points in from a particular viewpoint, for example, fly in from the left. However, if this is done then all the slides should use the same effect, again consistency gives a more professional appearance. Spacing between bullet points is also important so that they are clearly separate, and if at different levels, it is clear which groups belong to the level above.

—— A sample presentation ——

For our sample presentation, we will consider that the hall hire (mentioned in the last two chapters) has been taking place for a whole year and the treasurer needs to present the results to the committee so that the business can be reviewed.

We will go through the stages that are typical for creating a slide show and also consider the features that we will need in the presentation graphics software to achieve the required result.

The first stage is to decide in outline the various messages/points that need to be put across to our audience. We could just list these on a piece of paper, crossing out or changing our list as necessary, however, it is much easier and more efficient to use an outline facility, which should be available in the presentation graphics software. This allows us to build up the presentation as a series of headings and points as different levels.

For example, perhaps during the year the membership of the committee changed and the new members need to be informed about the background to the project. We can create an outline for the background slide and then continue to build outlines for each of the points on the background slide as shown in figure 4.1.

---

1 ⊟ Background to Hall Hire Project

- Ideas behind project
- Objectives
- Aims for first year

2 ⊟ Ideas Behind Project

- Obtain revenue for new equipment
- Provide facilities for local groups
- Minimise capital expenditure
- Use existing facilities fully

3 ⊟ Objectives

- Maintain hall and ancillary facilities
- Achieve a profit on the hall hire business
- Achieve a reputation for low-cost, reliable, helpful services

4 ⊟ Aims for First Year

- Balance books/achieve a small profit
- Obtain regular customers
- Learn the business

Figure 4.1 Outline of presentation

The treasurer will continue to build up the presentation in this way, bringing in data/graphs from the spreadsheets and perhaps examples of documents or parts of documents from the word processing work.

——— Building a presentation ———

In this section, we will take part of the treasurer's presentation and build it as a series of slides. We will explain the design considerations and the ideas behind each slide.

Having decided on the content of the presentation by using the outline facility, the next step is to decide on the look of the slides. There may be a standard style for your company or you may be designing your own styles. Generally, you will want a consistent style for the title and for the body containing the text. This can be achieved easily if a master slide facility is available which will have a template containing all the formatting settings associated with it.

The template will contain settings for both the title and the body formats including:

- font types, sizes, styles (e.g. bold, italic) and colour for the text;
- framing of the text with shapes, colour, patterns, shadowing;
- indentations and bullet points for the body text.

By selecting the appropriate master, the look of the slides is automatically set but can be changed by highlighting the individual parts of the slide and changing them as required.

The treasurer's report is intended to put across the essential points on the results of the first year of the hall hire project. We have avoided using clip art and drawn shapes as these could distract attention from the main messages in this case, although these could be useful for emphasis for a different presentation.

Figure 4.2 Heading slide with shadowed box

The first slide of the presentation shows the main heading in a simple shadowed box (figure 4.2). If the business had a logo, this could be added to the master slide so that it would appear on every slide. The next and following slides would appear in the form shown in figure 4.3. These consist of a heading or title and bullet points for the text.

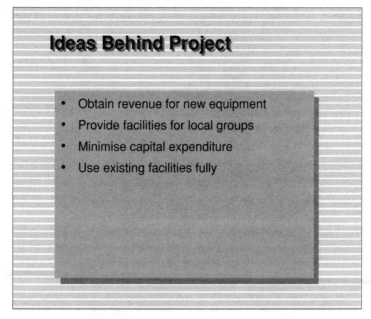

Figure 4.3 Slide with heading and bullet points

In this presentation, the treasurer will want to bring in data in the form of spreadsheets or graphs. Figure 4.4 shows the Income for the year as a bar chart imported from the spreadsheet package.

Often when a presentation is given, the audience wants to copy down the information on the slides to take away with them. It is useful to have a facility to print out the slides, several to a page, to hand out to the audience, as shown in figure 4.5. Also, the presenter may want to to have some notes as a prompt for his talk, and these may be added to slides and printed as shown in figure 4.6.

When giving the presentation it is useful to show more information progressively instead of all the points on a slide at once. This may be done by creating build slides so that bullet points are shown one at a

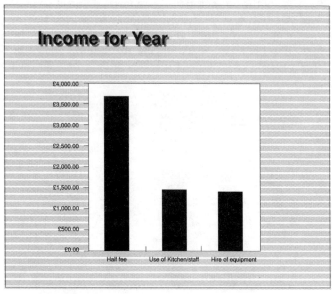

Figure 4.4 Imported bar chart

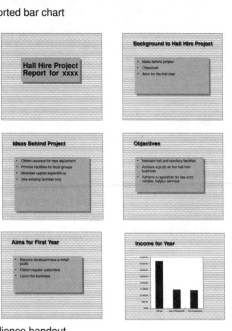

Figure 4.5 Audience handout

Notes for presentation

1. The hall hire project has been going for a whole year now. The purpose of this presentation is to go through a review of the business.

2. I will start with the ideas behind the project as I know several of you are new to the committee. Then I will outline our original objectives and aims.

3. The main part of the talk will be concerned with factual information of our income and expenditure.

4. Finally, I will discuss whether our aims have been met and ask you to express your views.

Figure 4.6 Slide with notes

time with the previous bullet points on the slide being dimmed or changing in colour. The bullet points can be made to fly in from different directions, for example, by choosing 'Fly From Left', as each bullet point appears it will come in from the left of the screen.

—— Summary of features required ——

A good presentation graphics package will need the following features:

- *Slide creation in both outline and singly*: as mentioned previously, the outline feature allows you to build up a series of slides quickly. You can then make changes, move slides around, and change the level of the points. Creating slides singly gives you a better feel for the amount of information you should put on one slide and how it will look. You can start to experiment with font styles and sizes, different bullet points, etc.

- *Slide changer and slide sort viewer*: a slide changer allows you to move through the slides backwards and forwards, while the slide sort viewer allows you to see a screenful, of small views of the slides at a time, making it easy to move slides to different positions and to select the slide to be changed.
- *Drawing tools*: it is useful to be provided with a set of shapes that allow you to create some simple diagrams and to add text to these.
- *Font and bullet point selection*: you should be able to choose from a comprehensive list of font styles and sizes for your text and also different bullet point styles, for example, solid circles and squares, stars, ticks.
- *Data sheets and graphs*: you may want to import data and graphs from your spreadsheet package but it is also useful to be able to create data tables and graphs from within the presentation graphics package.
- *Clip art*: a comprehensive range of clip art will allow you to add pictures, arrows, etc., without having to draw these yourself. You should be able to size these and move them to any part of the slide.
- *Templates*: in a professional slide show there should be consistency of appearance between all the slides and this can be achieved by the use of templates. By selecting a template and applying this to the whole of the slide show, all the formatting, colour and other style features will be the same throughout.
- *Notes and handouts*: The notes feature allows you to to add notes to each slide which you can then print for your reference when giving your talk. You may also want to give handouts of the slides, with or without the notes, to your audience; it is useful if several slides can be printed on one page.
- *Slide master*: this facility allows you to make changes in format on the slide master and then apply it to the whole slide show.
- *Progressive disclosure slides*: this facility allows you to gradually bring in your bullet points, while changing the colour or fading out previous bullet points on the slide. The direction in which the bullet points come in may also be selectable.

Presentation methods

The presentation methods largely depend on the technology available in the room used for giving the presentation. At the simplest level, the presentation slides can be output onto acetate film, as mentioned previously. The disadavantage of this method is that the acetates have to be manually changed on the overhead projector, sometimes requiring a second person to do this. The task is made easier if the acetates are bound into a special book which clips onto the overhead projector. They can then be flipped over more easily although in a fixed order.

For a large audience, most lecture rooms will be provided with a 35 mm slide projector. The slides will need to be made up and then placed in a carousel which the speaker can rotate clockwise and anti-clockwise using a hand-held device.

Output direct from the computer can be achieved simply by plugging the computer into a large monitor which can be viewed by, say, six to eight people. You can also arrange to have a number of monitors daisy-chained together and placed in different parts of the room for wider viewing. Projection onto a wall-mounted or portable large screen can be achieved by the use of an LCD panel placed on the top of an overhead projector. The latter needs to be powerfully-lit and the room usually has to be darkened.

Some very good portable, although relatively expensive, equipment is now available that allows output direct from the computer to be viewed onto a screen in ordinary light. Often large lecture rooms will have an RGB (red/green/blue) projector built in which gives an excellent large image on a screen.

The advantage of using output directly from the computer is that the speaker has full control of the movement from one slide to another. Full use of the slide build facility can be made and it is also easy to move back to a previous slide if necessary. For some purposes it is useful to have a continuously running slide show and a large monitor will usually be used for this.

5
SECURITY AND PROTECTION OF DATA

— Vulnerability of computer data —

Computer data is vulnerable in a number of ways which can be categorised as follows:

- unauthorised access to data
- loss of data
- corruption of data.

Data needs to be protected against unauthorised access for many different reasons. The data may comprise sensitive information about a person's health (through his or her medical records) or financial affairs (banking, insurance records, etc.), or about a company's products and plans, to give just a few examples. In these cases, it is important to prevent unauthorised users, both within and outside the organisation holding the data, gaining access to read or change the information, or to transfer it to other computer systems.

Inadequate protection could result in the possibility of criminal activity such as blackmail, fraud, theft and industrial espionage, or financial loss or other serious misuse of data, for example, access to a country's defence information. Examples of people (hackers) gaining unauthorised access to information on large computer networks have been reported in the media. Specialist companies have been set up to combat computer hacking, and they advise on measures that should be put in place to make data as secure as possible.

Computer data can be lost through different circumstances. During the creation of the data, the user can accidentally 'wipe out' the data by, for example, deleting sections of a document, spreadsheet or database entry. There may be a power failure or somebody may accidentally pull out a plug, resulting in the loss of the data currently in the computer's memory.

Another way that data may be lost occurs if there is a hardware or software failure. This can happen again when the data is being worked on or after the data has been saved if, for example, a hard disk fails or is destroyed.

Data may also be lost or corrupted deliberately by people introducing viruses. The possibility of this has increased since the advent of personal computers and the many free disks available to users.

We will look at each of these hazards in turn to see what is being done and can be done to protect computer data from loss and corruption.

The privacy of personal data on individuals is an issue that has been addressed by many countries through legislation. It is important that individuals know what information is held on them to ensure that this is correct. Transfer of information between countries may be inhibited if one of the countries does not have appropriate data protection legislation. This can severely restrict an organisation's activities and hence observing this type of legislation has become essential for major trading companies.

— Preventing unauthorised access —

A large computer or network of computers may need to be accessed by many users. Not all the users will need access to all the data or to all the system's facilities. This means that valid users will each have a profile against their identification code (name, account number) which gives details of their privileges. These will specify the parts of the system and resources allocated to them. They may only be allowed to access part of the total database or be allowed to read data but not change it or add to it; they may only be allowed to use certain programs and certain computers on the network, have limitations on the amount of disk space available to them and may be restricted as to which printers they can use.

To gain access to these privileges, the user will need to enter a password in addition to his or her identification code. This password is personal to the user and needs to be kept secret.

When new users are first set up with a list of privileges by the system administrator, they will be given a password. The first thing that they will be advised to do is to log into the system with their identification code and password and to immediately change their password. Often this is done by typing in the new password once and then again to confirm it. The password will not appear on the screen but be shown by, say, a series of asterisks.

The user should keep this new password completely secret and change it frequently to prevent other people gaining access to the system, and to the user's privileges, by using his or her identification code and password, if the latter has been written down or chosen inappropriately. The passwords chosen should not be obvious, such as the user's name, to prevent an unauthorised person gaining entry by easily guessing passwords.

Various techniques have been devised to prevent and detect fraudalent use of a computer system. For example, attempts to break into the system by trial and error methods can be detected by recording each entry type, time of day, terminal or PC used, and user, when logging in and out of the system, including whether a correct or incorrect password was given. This information can be checked by the organisation's security officer and users, so that they can check the use that has been made of their files. Wide publicity should be given of the existence of such a security system to deter unauthorised users from attempting to break into the computer system.

A technique such as cryptography may be used to conceal information stored in the computer (such as passwords and sensitive data) or during transmission of data over telephone lines (in case the lines are tapped). Commonly used methods encode the information so that it cannot be read without the key for decoding it. The transformation of the information may be carried out by the software or hardware. Sophisticated methods tend to be costly and are used for especially sensitive data.

As far as stand-alone personal computers are concerned, the main protection is clearing information from the screen and locking disks and tapes away. Some PCs have a key to prevent the hard disk being accessed in the computer or the disk may be removable so can be taken out and locked up when required.

If a computer is exchanged for, say, a more powerful model, the user should make sure that all the data required is saved on the network, or on tapes or disks, and then reformat the hard disk to wipe the information from it. Otherwise the new user will have access to any information that had been saved on the hard disk (just deleting it is not enough). The same applies to tapes and disks that have been used as back-ups before discarding them.

Preventing loss of data

We have already mentioned some of the ways in which computer data can be lost; now we will look at ways of preventing this loss.

First, when creating data, it is important to save your work as you proceed. For example, if you are using a WP package, you may be able to set this so that it automatically saves your work onto the hard disk at intervals. You should also save sections as you create them so that if, say, there is a power cut or the system fails for some reason, the amount of work lost is minimal and can easily be entered again later. Similarly, at an appropriate stage, it is a good idea to save your work onto a floppy disk or elsewhere on the network as a back-up copy.

If you are working on a network, then the system administrator will have a system in place for backing up all the files on the network. Depending on the amount of data and its sensitivity and importance, the period between full back-ups will vary. There may be a system of partial back-ups taken at regular, short intervals which result in a full back-up being available over a longer interval.

The system adminstrator may decide to back up all essential information very often and the less important information less frequently. If you are creating important information yourself, you can make yourself responsible for backing it up if it is personal to you. However, if the information is important for your organisation, the back-up procedures should be discussed with your system administrator as it will impact on your organisation.

The back-up tapes and disks need to be held securely. Those that hold essential information need to be locked away in fireproof safes, perhaps in a different building from the computer system. It is important to be aware that although computer equipment has become very reliable, disasters can occur, for example, through a hardware or software failure destroying information on a hard disk. The resultant loss of data can have serious consequences for an organisation if back-up procedures are inadequate or have not been followed correctly.

Protection against corruption of data

Sometimes corruption of data can be more serious than loss of data because it is less obvious. If data is lost it is often noticed quickly and, providing good back-up procedures are in place, remedial action can be taken quickly.

Data can be corrupted by software or hardware errors, mistakes by users or by deliberate intervention. Usually, but not always, data corrupted through software or hardware not working as it should shows up in an obvious way because it is likely that the results will be completely wrong. Perhaps some circumstances have not been allowed for in the software and these will need to be corrected and the computer runs repeated. These sorts of errors should be highlighted when checks are made on the results.

Checking results is an important aspect of working with computers. Mistakes can and do occur, particularly when new software is introduced. Since computer programs are written by people, mistakes (bugs) can be introduced and it is very difficult, if not impossible, for software manufacturers to test every combination of circumstances that the software can be used for by the end users. It is always a good idea to do some checking yourself so that you are satisfied that you are using the software correctly and that it is giving the right results.

The trend in businesses is to work on networks of computers and share access to databases. This way of working can give rise to more data files becoming corrupted if write permission (the ability for a user to change, delete or add information) is given to too many or the wrong users and if there is a lack of training on how the systems should be used.

Some monitoring is also important to enable quick remedial action to be taken should data become corrupted for whatever reason. An example could be where a number of people need to add information to a 'contacts' database. If a user lacks expertise or care he/she could easily delete or change a record accidentally and perhaps be unaware that it has occurred. For such a system, it may be advisable to restrict the number of people who can change the database but allow read-only access to everybody in the company.

The deliberate corruption of data is often through the introduction of viruses. A virus is a software routine written by a programmer with malicious intent to disrupt or destroy work on your computer. Once a virus is in your computer, it may be difficult to eliminate it.

The damage that the virus does may be limited, for example, a message may appear on your screen announcing itself, or disastrous by wiping out all the information from your hard disk. The virus may spread from one computer to other computers on the network, or through exchange of floppy disks, doing untold damage, so protection is essential.

The first line of defence is to use special virus-checking software to check every floppy disk received from outside sources. Many organisations now have a rule that every floppy disk that comes in from whatever source must go to the systems department for virus checking.

Also, it is a good idea to virus check your computer system regularly to ensure that no known viruses have been introduced. If you are on a network, your systems department may run software on a regular basis which checks your PC for viruses, so that every few days, say, as soon as you log onto the network, the virus checker will come into play.

Virus checking software is continually being updated as new viruses are discovered, and often sold on a subscription basis so that users receive updates. The virus checking should be very comprehensive so can typically take ten minutes to check your PC's hard disk. It is a problem that needs to be taken very seriously since so much important information is now stored on computer networks.

—— Data protection legislation ——

The increase in data processing activity, with many organisations holding personal data on networks of PCs as well as on a central database, has created more complex problems in ensuring the accuracy of the information and limiting access to it. The processing of personal data, its use, and access to it by individuals has to be controlled according to the requirements of data protection legislation. Each country has its own regulations, so only some general principles are discussed here.

All data processing/computer systems in an organisation holding personal data need to be registered with the Registrar. The registration includes such details as the purposes for which the system is to be used, the data held on it, any linkages to other systems involving transfer, or access to, personal data, how long the data is to be held (retention time), who will use the data and when it will be used. Organisations must also provide adequate back-up of data files, and state the security measures for restricting access to the data.

The register is made available to the general public and individuals can request to see the information held on them in particular data files; a fee may have to be paid for this service. the organisation then has a duty to supply this information in a form that is intelligible to the individual. This is important as much of the information may be held in coded form in the computer files.

The Registrar has to ensure that registered organisations comply with the legislation. Possible sanctions against organisations not fulfilling their obligations include fines and de-registration, resulting in transfer of information being prohibited.

This is the basis of the type of data protection legislation which has the following purposes. As well as ensuring the free flow of information between countries, the intention of such legislation is to establish the principle that personal information held on computer files can be inspected and corrected by the individual concerned as a right, with some exceptions, for example, in the case of national security.

6

LINKING WITH THE
OUTSIDE WORLD

— Local and wide area networks —

Today it is becoming rarer for people to work in isolation on their own PCs. There is a great deal of information held on computers that is useful and easily accessible to PC users.

You may be working in a business or educational environment with required/permitted access to databases holding information about customers, products, students, rooms, equipment. You may be using this information to create reports and analyses using word processing and spreadsheet packages, and perhaps preparing presentations on the results. For these types of uses you need to be linked into a network of computers and, in most instances, this will be a local area network (LAN) within your organisation.

All the computers on the LAN will be linked together by special cable, depending on the network being used, and you will need a network card in your PC with a connector to the network cable. If your computer is of the notebook type, the network card is likely to be a PCMCIA card which slots into the computer and is readily removable if you want to put in a different PCMCIA card.

Most notebook computers will have two slots for PCMCIA cards so you can use the other slot for, say, a fax/modem card, which you can use for communicating with wide area networks (WANs) over the telephone. Your desktop PC may also use an internal fax/modem card or an external modem box.

— Networks within an organisation —

Your local area network will have one or more file servers on it and one or more printer servers (see figure 6.1). The file servers will be large PCs or more powerful computers capable of handling access to and from all the end user (client) PCs for data processing applications. The file servers control access to and from large amounts of network disk storage of programs and data files. The printer servers handle all printing requests as required.

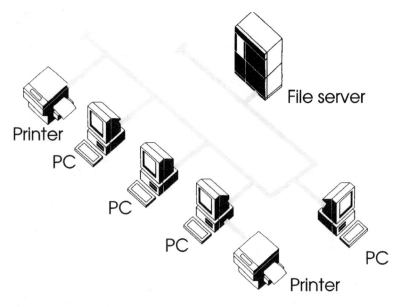

Figure 6.1 A Local Area Network (LAN)

Typically, a user will log on to the network with his name and password and then bring up a windows environment showing all the application programs as icons. He can then choose the program he wants to work with and save his work either locally on his PC's hard disk or more often, perhaps, on one or more of the network disk drives which have been allocated to his department. The disk directory structure will have been set up in consultation with the rest of his department so that each member uses the same conventions for storing information.

There will be areas on the allocated disk drives for holding shared information and personal information. The user will have access to local printers in his department but some of the more specialised printers, for example, for printing in colour, may be located outside his department. He will have been given access to certain computers and resources, for example, an amount of disk space on the network, and can work with any of these computers and application programs allocated to him.

External links

The method of linking to external computer systems depends basically on whether you are linking direct from your PC or via your organisation's LAN.

If you are linking direct, then you will use your modem or fax/modem plugged into a telephone socket. You will select the appropriate software program from your windows environment which will have a facility for inputting the number to be dialled and initiating the connection to a particular external system. Once you are connected you will gain access to the system by the normal name/password method. When you have finished you log out and disconnect.

If you are linking through your organisation's LAN, you should be able to select the appropriate icon without dialling from your local phone but letting the network make the connection.

The phone lines you use may be on the ordinary public telephone network or may be private leased lines where a rental is paid for the lines but not for the calls, making it more cost-effective for, say, frequent communication between an organisation's different offices. Communication between sites in different countries is likely to involve satellites and services may be provided at local telephone charges even though the communication is over a long distance.

A typical office example

To illustrate the use of an office network system, we will look at the work of a manager in a sales organisation.

When he comes into the office in the morning, he will connect his computer to the organisation's LAN by plugging his network card connector into the network cable, switch on his computer and choose the option to link into the office network, and log on with his name and password.

From the windows environment, he will choose the electronic mail (e-mail) icon and log into this with his name and the same or different password. Any mail that has come in for him since he last logged in will come up as a list for him to select the item and read it.

He can view each mail on the screen, elect to reply to it with copies to other users (including himself), forward the mail to other people and/or transfer it to his e-mail mailboxes. He will have organised the mailboxes in folders for easy access. For example, he may have a folder called 'products' and within that have mailboxes for each of the products that the company sells, so that information from mails about certain products are all filed in one place. He may have another folder called 'team' which has mailboxes for each member of his team.

Having read and dealt with all his outstanding mail, he may have noted that reception had sent him mail messages to inform him that faxes have come in for him. These will have been directed straight to his computer. He can now call up the fax program (by clicking on the fax icon), access the faxes, print them if required, prepare replies using standard fax templates on the network and the WP software and send them to the recipients through the fax program, all without moving from his PC.

He may, alternatively, allocate the faxes for reply by mailing messages and forwarding the faxes to his staff. Perhaps a fax required some action such as processing an order; whoever is replying to this can call up other template forms, transfer the details onto these and then forward the forms electronically to the administration department for invoicing and to the despatch department for sending out the products. The ease of communication makes for speedy and accurate transfer of information, resulting in increased customer satisfaction, as the products requested will be despatched very quickly, and likely increased cash flow as the invoice will also be despatched quickly for payment.

Some of the e-mails will be concerned with flow of information, perhaps on the development of products or answers to queries. If it is an international company, there will be easy communication between the organisation's different offices and worldwide distributors, without having to take into account time differences, as the mails will be stored until the recipients log in and read them.

In the meantime, consultants in the company may have been busy carrying out data processing projects for their international clients and sending databases via e-mail to them. This can be done quickly, efficiently and securely by compressing the data to a compact form and using encryption. This transfer of data can be achieved via the Internet, which is discussed in the next section.

— The Internet and World Wide Web —

The Internet is a system of interconnecting computer networks giving access to a vast amount of information to millions of users in the home, in schools/colleges/universities and in businesses, on a worldwide basis.

We will look at the type of information available, who provides this, and how you can gain access to it. A complete description of the Internet and its use is given in *Teach Yourself the Internet* by Mac Bride.

Access to the Internet is through a modem and telephone line, as explained in chapter 1. Many businesses and most colleges/universities provide access through their local area networks. Individual users can gain access through service providers. The latter will have nodes in certain cities and users can dial in to their nearest node so reducing telephone charges.

There are many ways of using the Internet. We have already talked about sending/receiving messages and data files through the e-mail facility on the Internet. You can also download programs, text and graphics, look at pictures from exhibitions/museums, access information held in libraries and search for particular topics and papers, join in group discussions or games, and much more.

Millions of pages of information are available on the World Wide Web stored on host computers throughout the world. These can be accessed through a connection with a service provider and a program called a Web browser. The latter allows you to find the Web pages that you are interested in and display them on your computer's screen with graphics and sound (provided you have graphics/sound hard-ware/software on your computer). Just a word of caution; it is easy to spend a great deal of time browsing through the information because there may be much to interest you, but all the time you will be running up a telephone bill. It is better to focus on a particular area that you want to follow up and narrow the the amount of searching that you need to do. We will illustrate this with some examples.

Searching for information

The first step in accessing information on the World Wide Web (WWW) is to call up the browser installed on your system by clicking on the appropriate icon. This may bring up the home page of your service provider or your organisation's home page as the starting point (see figure 6.2).

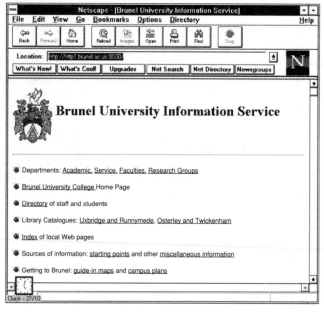

Figure 6.2 An Internet home page

Within a home page, you will find a list of subjects which are links to other pages. By moving the cursor to any of these and clicking you will gain access to the linked page. In this way you can explore different subjects to the depth that you require. For example, you may be interested in travel. You can gain access to information on airlines, timetables and travel agencies in particular countries and locations. Once you have arrived at the page giving the detailed information that you are looking for, you can note this down or print it out.

You may need to access these pages on a regular basis if you are a frequent traveller in which case you would want to go straight to the relevant pages in one step. You can do this by creating a bookmark which stores the location of the page with its title. The next time you want to access that page all you have to do is to view your bookmarks and click on the one referring to the section you wish to access.

Types of information

The owners of the factual information contained in WWW pages will update this as required. If the information refers to products, for example, the suppliers will want to make sure that potential buyers of the products will have the latest details.

A computer manaufacturer may want to publicise some of the latest technology with papers comprising many Web pages of technical information. The date when the file was last updated will be displayed together with an Internet address for comments. Other information, such as entries in encyclopaedias, will be more static and will rarely be updated with new facts.

Some information will only last for a short time. An example of this is the publication of events. Perhaps you are interested in going to a jazz festival; a search for this may come up with a list of locations with dates and prices and an Internet address for enquiries.

Another travel example uses a database and a program to provide you with answers to queries on the quickest way to travel between two locations on the London Underground. You can put in the names of the stations or names of well-known places or grid references from a London street guide. It will then give you a best travel route showing the time between stations and where to change on to different underground lines.

Sharing information

One of the aims of the Internet is to allow people with common interests to exchange ideas and generally communicate with each other. If you know people's Internet addresses you can send e-mail to them. You can also join newsgroups when you will receive articles written by members and you can contribute articles yourself.

Another way of sharing information is to become a member of a forum. This will mean that you will get all the messages sent to the forum and you can also send messages to the forum members by e-mailing to the forum name. This is a useful method for businesses to inform their employees and their clients about products and events through the Internet.

Creating your own Web pages

Your service provider may allow you to have your own Web pages free or at a low cost. This will give you the opportunity of creating your own home page which you can set up with links to other Web pages. Creating Web pages requires some technical expertise but is worthwhile particularly for organisations wishing to promote their products or services.

7

INTEGRATED BUSINESS SYSTEMS

Introduction

The simple use of computers to process information held in a single file, such as a names and addresses, has led to more ambitious applications as the technology has developed. Today most business applications are integrated applications consisting of a suite of several files from which data can be extracted and merged into reports, screen displays, etc. The ability to network computers, either locally, or around the world means that the users of the system can be using a common database. Thus not only is the data integrated but also the activities of the users.

The organisation of the data and the design of the data files are crucial in their subsequent use, regardless of the application. Files of data held in an organised way form a database. This chapter discusses some of the typical issues in developing database systems and retrieving information. The chapter concludes by describing the elements of an integrated accounting system and also an interactive sales system.

Typical processing of data

Simple computer files can be likened to a card index system. Individual cards making up the file are records. Thus a personnel file consists of personnel records whereby each record relates to one individual. The organisation of this data will be covered in the next section. Assuming the design of the system allows the data to be organised correctly there are a number of typical processing stages that are undertaken in most if not all systems.

It is important that any system is up to date and this requires that once records are created they are maintained. Databases therefore require menu options allowing the user to:

1 add new records
2 delete records
3 amend details within a record
4 restructure the file.

This last requirement, whereby you already have a file, but you now want to 'redesign' it and maybe attach additional information to the records can present problems. With very simple systems you might have to start again and create the new file from scratch but the more elaborate database systems will allow additional information to be incorporated. The restructuring of a database is therefore not undertaken lightly. It is best if the database is planned and designed to cover future requirements at the start.

The above maintenance options only keep the database up to date and relevant. The database is there to be used and to do that you need to be able to:

1 search the database to extract appropriate information
2 create reports, as required
3 extract selective information and transfer as input to other
   applications.

Searching for and extracting data allows queries to be answered immediately on a day to day basis. Reporting options allow lists to be produced for meetings or incorporation into word processed reports (see figure 7.1). Transferring selected data to produce secondary data files (known as exporting) allows these files to become the input to be processed further by, for example, statistical, presentation or modelling packages.

A computer can only calculate and manipulate data very quickly, the effectiveness of the application depends upon the design and setting up of the files into an appropriate database.

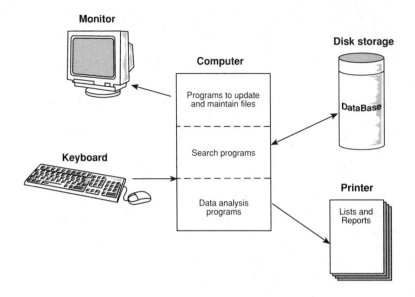

Figure 7.1 Processing using a database

Organisation of data

The basis of any database application as previously described are the records. The data within a record is held in a field and these fields are standardised throughout a file. For example, a file of book references might consist of the following five fields for each record:

Field 1   Author's name(s)
Field 2   Book title
Field 3   Publisher
Field 4   Year of publication
Field 5   Price

In terms of data storage each field in a record will consist of a certain number of characters (the letters A to Z, numbers and other symbols from the keyboard). A space counts as a character. In the case of the first field, the author's names, 'Blogg J' would count as 7 characters, and 'Smith P and Peach F D' would be 21 characters. Thus the number of characters required for a particular field entry varies. Some database systems allow fields to be of varying length but others require the maximum size of a field to be stipulated at the design stage. In this case the entry is then padded out with spaces when the data is stored so that the author's name always requires 30 characters, say, to be stored in a record. This is termed a fixed length field.

If a system uses fixed length fields then the size of the field, which is set at the record design stage, needs to anticipate the largest entry that is likely to be required. Once designed and in use any subsequent requirement to modify a field length would entail redesigning the file and copying all the existing entries over into the new file. This can be a major task and emphasises the importance of designing the initial file correctly.

Users of databases usually want any information that is extracted to be in say, alphabetic order. Superficially this requires that the records in the database have to be constantly sorted and moved around to insert a new entry into its 'proper' position. In practice most databases store the records in a first come first stored position, the newest record to be added to the end of the current database. Outputting the records in a particular sequence is achieved by means of additional index files. Reading an index file sequentially 'tells' the computer which is the next record number to be accessed. For example, consider a book reference database containing just the following six records:

Record 1	Smith J	........etc.
Record 2	Edgar P	........etc.
Record 3	Adams K	........etc.
Record 4	Brown G	........etc.
Record 5	Tilly T	........etc.
Record 6	Baker J	........etc.

An index file consisting simply of the six numbers, 3, 6, 4, 2, 1, 5 indicates the sequence the records should be accessed or printed in order to produce an alphabetic sequence. A similar index file could indicate the sequence required to output the records in alphabetic book title sequence. It is much easier to rearrange and sort an index file than move all the record details around in the database.

The index of index files can also be used to link two data files so that record number 3 in the book reference data file could be linked to record number 12 say, in a library user file.

Another method used to read records in a file in a different sequence to which they are stored is to use pointers. In this method each record has a field (the pointer) which contains the record number of the next record to be read to follow a specified sequence.

Data entry, screen layout and design

The screen is used to display information retrieved from files and also to display entries from the keyboard, or other devices, when data is entered. The field entry positions on the screen need to be distinguished from the screen background and the title of the field displayed alongside. This data entry screen becomes a mask that ensures all the records have the same formats.

Jumping between fields is often possible by pressing a particular key, usually the Tab key. Thus successive pressing of the Tab key cycles the user through each field in turn. Often pressing the Tab key and another key, e.g. the Alt key, will cause the cursor to cycle through the fields in the opposite direction.

Within any one application it is preferable that the use of these special keys has the same consistent effect. It is also preferable in developing a system that the action of the special keys and other screen displays are consistent with the conventions used by the operating system or shell, e.g. Windows. In practice many of the systems used to develop the screen displays in applications (development systems) automatically adhere to the appropriate operating system conventions.

When data is entered into a system there might be checks carried out to ensure that as far as possible the data is valid. For example checks may be built in to ensure that alphabetic characters cannot be entered into a numeric field and vice versa, dates might be checked for the correct format, etc.

Check digits are sometimes used with numeric data to ensure that the number has been correctly entered. This system is used with ISBNs allocated to books. Each book published has a unique ISBN (International Standard Bibliography Number) whose last character is a check digit. The ISBN of the first edition of this book (*Teach Yourself Computers and their Use*) is 0-340-35652-9. The last digit (9) is the check digit and the arithmetic process applied to the preceding numbers should result in the answer 9. Starting with the penultimate digit (2), each digit is successively multiplied by 2, 3, 4, 5, etc. and these weighted multiples totalled, i.e.

$$2 \times 2 = 4$$
$$5 \times 3 = 15$$
$$6 \times 4 = 24$$
$$5 \times 5 = 25$$
$$3 \times 6 = 18$$
$$0 \times 7 = 0$$
$$4 \times 8 = 32$$
$$3 \times 9 = 27$$

Total = 145

This total is divided by 11 and the remainder noted. In this case 13 with a remainder of 2. The remainder (2) is then subtracted from 11 to provide the check digit, i.e. $11 - 2 = 9$. Because of the use which is made of 11 in this procedure this method is known as the modulus 11 check digit system. If the book's ISBN number was incorrectly entered by say, the transposing of digits, the calculation would not agree with the check digit of 9 and the ISBN would be rejected by the computer.

Other types of checks would include range checks. For example, days ought to lie between 1 and 31, and months between 1 and 12. If the range of entries to a field is limited to say, one of four possibilities, then the system might display the choice while that field is accessed. In a windows based system the choice might be made by clicking on the chosen item from the list. This approach prevents unacceptable responses being made.

At the data entry stage the data is usually only written to the files when all the data has been entered, displayed on the screen and a key pressed to acknowledge that no further editing is required. Until the screen is accepted in this manner the data can be altered and corrected, usually by moving around the screen and over-typing.

Sometimes the number of fields and the amount of data to be entered necessitates more than one data entry screen. In this case the sequence of data entry screens might be determined by information entered on a previous screen. The system should also provide a way of aborting the current screen and 'backtracking' to earlier screens. This is often achieved by pressing the Escape key.

—— Searching for information ——

The ability to search for information is fundamental in a database system. Most systems offer the means of browsing, that is accessing the next record, but generally this is an inefficient way of finding information.

Some systems, where the range of possible searches is limited, might offer the choice via a screen menu. More elaborate search systems are likely to present a blank record (a blank search mask) on the screen for the user to fill in whatever search criterion is required in the appropriate fields.

The search criterion is expressed as a 'logical' statement, using either words or mathematical symbols. Typical elements of a search statement would be:

equal to	=
greater than	>
less than	<
greater than or equal to	> = (alternative, = >)
less than or equal to	< = (alternative, = <)

Thus the search entry in a Year of Publication field in a bibliographic database might contain:

    greater than 1992
or > 1992.

This would specify all books published in 1993 and later. If the selection is to be narrowed further to only books authored by Brown then the author field might contain:

    equal to Brown
or = Brown
or Brown.

The last example, using just the name, is possible in some systems as 'equal to' can be assumed if a blank search mask is being used.

Some systems require the search criteria to be entered in the form of a sentence containing 'and' and/or 'or'. The previous example would be expressed as follows:

    if Year is greater than 1992 and Author is equal to 'Brown'

With this style of search any specified text usually has to be included within single quotes to distinguish it from the logic statement. An example of using 'or' might be where the search is for two authors, e.g.

if Year > 1992 and Author = 'Brown' or Author = 'Jones'

Note that the field name has to be specified with every instance of search criteria. Development of compound search statements needs careful thought as the mixing of 'and's and 'or's can have unintended effects.

Another feature that is often implemented is the ability to search for a character sequence known as a string of text within the complete field. This requirement is usually indicated by the use of special characters within the text. Thus Author = 'Brown' searches for a precise match and only finds Brown but Author = 'Brown*', say, finds any name beginning with Brown and would also select Browning for example. Here, the asterisk is termed a 'wildcard'.

A convention using wildcards has developed within computer systems and may be used within database systems as part of the searching procedure. Two symbols are traditionally used as wildcards, ? and *.

The idea is that a wildcard is used to signify unspecified characters in a field (or filename). The ? character is used to represent individual 'missing' characters, so a search for 'Br???' is essentially a search for a five-character entry beginning with Br. Five-character names such as Brown, Brett and Bruce would be found by this search but not Browning. The ? character can be used anywhere in the entry so that '?im' might find Jim and Tim (but not Timothy).

The * character used as a wildcard represents any number of unknown characters and therefore is only used at the end of a specification, e.g. 'Br*'. A search using 'Br*' would encompass Brown, Browning, Brocket, Brian, Brick, etc., in fact any entry beginning with Br.

A further aspect of using search options is whether the system is case sensitive, i.e. distinguishes between upper and lower case letters. If the system is case sensitive the search criteria must be specified more carefully, e.g. a search for Mcdonald will not find McDonald.

It is important that a user of a system has a full understanding how the search options have been implemented and of any restrictions.

Updating and maintaining databases

Any database requires maintaining if it is not to become out of date. Records in a database might be changed or added to as and when necessary or they might be batched together and the system updated once a day, weekly or monthly. Accountancy systems often include files that are updated as and when together with files that are updated at the month's end.

It is important that the running and maintenance of a database system follows well defined procedures to preserve the integrity of the data. The first requirement is that failed transactions should never leave the database in an incorrect state. With multiple users the database should have good privacy and security features.

The privacy aspect is usually achieved by means of passwords to ensure only authorised users have access to appropriate parts of the system. The logging in and password system is usually based upon a hierarchical level of user access. The logging in characters (representing the user's identity) determines the level of access. The password can usually be changed at will by the user and so (in theory) is only known to themselves. As an added precaution when the password is entered via the keyboard it is not usually displayed on the screen.

When multiple users access a database over a network it is important that users can be temporarily 'locked out' of certain files if someone else is currently updating the file's records. If this was not done two users, for example, could be attempting to allocate the same remaining stock. In these situations it is important the 'locked out' user is informed via the screen as to what is happening and does not think the system has frozen or 'gone down'.

Provision also needs to be made for data recovery. The database hardware may suffer a power failure, or the file storage devices may fail. Regular back-ups of the database need to be made together with records of all the transactions made since the last back-up. The time between back-ups is a matter of judgement and depends upon the level of file activity. Files that are changed frequently need to be backed up more frequently. Some systems such as airline seat reservation systems may be backed up several times per hour so that in the event of a failure only the last few minutes have to be reconstructed.

The implementation and operation of good practice in a database system is usually the responsibility of one person, the data base administrator (DBA). In addition to ensuring that the database system runs smoothly the DBA's primary purpose is to ensure the system meets the users' requirements. The DBA will be responsible for maintaining the documentation in the system. This includes the preparation of a data dictionary that specifies details of the information to be found in the database.

———— Output and reports ————

The whole purpose of a database is to produce appropriate output when required. The output may be direct to the screen in response to an enquiry or be a report, listing or summarising information.

Output to the screen needs to also display field titles, etc. so that the information presented can be understood. The precise layout and presentation of screen displays may be stipulated as a series of menu options. In general, screen displays need to be predesigned when the system is developed.

Various printed reports may be predesigned and be available as menu options but in addition some systems allow content and layouts of reports to be specified at run time. This allows customised reports to be generated to meet particular circumstances. The option or module available for developing customised reports is sometimes referred to as a report generator. When extensive reports are produced there is a need to ensure that the output can be recognised and understood. Thus in addition to the basic information being produced the report needs to contain appropriate headers and titles and be dated. The pages should also be numbered. Other features that need to be available in generating reports include the ability to select and sort the selected entries into a prescribed order and also to perform simple calculations such as totalling columns of data.

The output need not be printed, instead it may be written to a file to become the input file in a suite of analysis programs. Thus the personnel database may be accessed to produce a file detailing length of service. This file could be the input to a statistical package that produces graphs and other statistics relating to the length of service of employees.

Careful thought is needed if the report options have to be decided at the systems design stage. The need for reports, their purpose and eventual use all need to be questioned. The frequency of generating the reports and their volume also need to be assessed. Producing routine reports from an ever-increasing size database can end up being very time-consuming and might lead to the need for faster output devices.

Accounting systems

Accounting is perhaps one of the most widely applied computer application areas. The range of accounting packages range from the very simple, suitable for a 'one man' business or club to very sophisticated systems integrated with payroll, stock keeping and other financial functions. Very few businesses write their own accounting system but rather use standard packages. The packages may be available as a series of modules, the company using whichever modules seem most suitable, e.g. nominal ledger, purchase ledger. This approach allows a basic accounting system to be set up and further modules added as required. However because the details of the accounting procedures vary between businesses most accounting packages allow for customisation.

While a fully integrated accounting system may have multiple users on-line to the database(s) the tradition of monthly statements and reports means that in practice many accounting systems consist of several files (ledgers) that are run independently. Information between these files are transferred (posted) on a batch basis, say once a week or month. Thus transactions relating to sales are entered in the sales ledger and purchase transactions to the purchase ledger. Information from these ledgers might then be posted to the nominal ledger monthly.

An accounting system when first purchased has to be set up. Information has to be filed as to the accounting periods (according to calendar months, four-week periods or other desired system). The number of VAT rates needs to be established and maybe a code associated with each rate. A system of codes needs to be devised for the ledger systems to cover types of sales, expenses, assets, income, and debtors. The need to report and control also means that cost centres need to be decided upon and identified by codes.

A small 'instant' print company uses the following analysis heading and codes in its sales ledger:

110501	Printing
110502	Photocopying
110503	Self-service
110504	Finishing
110505	Artwork
110506	Typesetting
110507	Colour photocopying
110508	Sundries
110509	Fax

The input to the sales ledger for a sales transaction will be the account number, invoice date and invoice number, item details and analysis code and appropriate VAT code. The sales ledger also contains details of payment received, e.g. account code, invoice number and payment made. In some systems the payment is associated with a particular invoice and the debt can be cancelled. With part payments and general payments 'on account' the balance has to be calculated at the end of the month to produce a statement. The sales ledger module's main task is therefore keeping a customer database up to date. The customer database in addition to containing the names and addresses of customers and details of outstanding payments needs to also record credit limits and settlements terms.

A purchase ledger operates in a similar fashion to a sales ledger except that the purchase ledger monitors the money owing and paid out to suppliers. Thus the purchasing module keeps a suppliers database up to date.

A third ledger, the nominal ledger, contains summarised details of the income and expenditure from the sales and purchase ledgers. In addition some data, such as rates, electricity, gas, etc. may be posted directly into the nominal ledger as they do not relate directly to a sale or purchase. This ledger is usually updated say at the month end to produce a variety of reports. Data from the sales ledger may be used to produce an aged debtors list giving the amounts overdue for 30, 60 and 90 days. This information is used by credit control to ensure that the company is not overlooking payments that are due and to chase up late payments. A similar age analysis of payments to be made from the purchase ledger helps in the development of cash flow budgets.

Another important output from the ledgers is a VAT analysis and summary. Further typical reports, produced say, quarterly, would include a profit and loss account, a balance sheet, and a trial balance.

In addition to the checks and controls required because the system is computerised, an accounting system needs to have other checking procedures in place. For example, invoices should not be payed to suppliers simply on presentation of an invoice. It is necessary to check the supplies have actually been received and are in good condition.

The complete failure of an accounting system could put a company out of business or serious errors in 'the books' could lead to disastrous management decisions. It is essential that adequate back-ups are made and that there is a well-planned recovery procedure. Access to the files should be closely controlled by passwords, etc. to ensure only authorised users can make changes to the databases. The system's transaction and analysis procedures need to be verified and the auditors will expect to be able to trace an entry and the consequences of any transaction through the system (the audit trail).

— A sales and marketing system —

Another type of integrated business system is one that can be used by a sales and administration team. It is based around a database of company records which is held on a networked file server accessible to the team from their PCs. Each time a new company becomes a prospective or actual client, a record is created containing a number of fields. The fields include the company name, address, telephone and fax numbers, name and position of the contacts, source of contact, type of organisation and status of company (client, prospect, supplier, etc.).

Account managers (the sales people) are allocated to the companies and their names are entered and also any notes, which can be added at any time when contact is made with the client. This means that the history of communications between the sales people and the clients/prospects is permanently recorded on hard disk for retrieval when required.

Another feature is an electronic calendar for recording appointments, reminders to make calls and to carry out tasks, which can be recorded when complete. Other people's calendars can be looked at when trying to arrange meetings. Various word processing templates can be linked to the system for producing different types of letters, faxes, labels, forms and reports.

The database can be searched for information by setting up search criteria with logical and/or statements. We can see how this system works in practice. Let us imagine we have a team of account managers who are selling computer software and have the support of a team of administrative staff.

A call comes in as an enquiry, perhaps in response to an advertisement, and is allocated to an account manager. He inputs the details direct into the database as a new record and makes some notes as to the requirements. A letter may be sent with an information pack in the first instance. The letter may be one of the standard ones or made up of standard and customised paragraphs. A label is printed, using the address already in the database, and the pack is sent off.

At a later stage, the account manager follows up the initial enquiry and tries to arrange a visit to give a presentation and demonstration of the products to the prospective client. The date of the visit is recorded in the calendar with a note regarding the purpose of the visit and perhaps the travel arrangements.

The visit is made and as a result a proposal or quotation is prepared by the account manager using a word processing package linked to the sales and marketing system. Again standard proposals and quotations are available on the file server hard disk and may be customised using the WP software.

The client accepts the proposal/quotation, perhaps after some further negotiations, and a request is put in to the administration department to raise a contract using a standard contract request form. This will automatically contain the client details, as pulled off the database by the system, the name of the account manager and date, so that only the specific product details, prices and any special conditions need to be entered by the account manager.

The contract is sent out, signed by the client and returned. The account manager now selects another form on the system to request that the software is sent out to the client; this is forwarded to the distribution department who make up the parcel and despatch it. Similar procedures are followed for existing clients ordering additional software.

Sales reports can be created from the recorded notes and analyses of software sales carried out. All these reports are set up by the database administrator, who ensures that the database is kept up to date and not cluttered up with obsolete files and records. He will also deal with loading of upgrades to the software and putting new users on, and trains the account managers and administrative staff, who also have access to the database, in the use of the system.

The account managers deal with clients in different cities all over the world so that when a visit is made further afield, it is more efficient to try to arrange more appointments in that city. It is an easy matter to set up search criteria which will select that account manager's clients and prospects in the city being visited and to print out the list of companies, addresses, telephone/fax numbers, contact names and notes. The account manager can then go through the list and phone people to make appointments, which are stored in the calendar. Travel and accommodation details are also recorded.

The account manager will take his notebook computer with him for the presentation and demonstrations and will want to have a version of the database on this. He carries out a synchronisation procedure while the notebook computer is attached to the network which results in the shared database on the network file server and on his notebook computer being updated so that they are identical. This means that the account manager has the latest version of the database on his notebook computer which he can update with information acquired during his visits. On returning to base, he will carry out the synchronisation process again so that his database and the network database become identically updated again.

While the account manager is away from his office, he may need to send and receive e-mail and faxes, and access external databases for information (either within the company or elsewhere). This can be achieved through the PCMCIA fax/modem card in his notebook computer when plugged into a telephone socket.

There are many other uses for the system. For example, seminars may be arranged to introduce new products. A mail-shot to invite clients to these can be produced through the system. First the invitations are set up as a document using the WP software. Then a selection of clients is made from the database using the appropriate search criteria. The mail-shot facility is used to merge the names and addresses of the selected clients with the invitation document so that a personalised letter can be printed for each client on the list. This can then be put into a window envelope and sent off. The whole process is thus easy and quick.

Using such a system increases the efficiency of the account managers and administrative staff making them more productive and successful.

8

SOME EVERYDAY USES FOR COMPUTERS

Introduction

Computers are used in business and commerce for a wide variety of applications. Many systems are based on large centralised computers (known as mainframes) which have fast processors, huge memory and disk storage capacities. The financial applications of large industrial companies are processed on these types of systems, as are the transactions carried out by banks, insurance companies and building societies.

The banking system has to process millions of cheques daily, so that a method for automatically reading cheques is essential. Similarly utilities, such as electricity and gas boards, need to produce bills and process accounts rapidly for their many customers. More convenient methods for obtaining cash from one's bank account (by the use of cash cards) and for paying bills (through viewdata systems) have been developed. The idea is to reduce the amount of paper being used and to eliminate postal charges where possible.

The retailing industry, with its huge turnover of many different items of goods, has used new technology to improve profitability and the service to its customers. Point of sale terminals are widely used in large stores, resulting in the capture of information that allows management to respond quickly to current situations. Other devices, such as hand-held data entry terminals and adapted television sets, enable representatives to enter orders quickly into their companies' computers over the public telephone system, and to send and receive messages using on-line systems such as the Internet.

Banking industry surveys have shown that of customers who stopped doing business with a particular organisation, 66% did so because of poor service. The importance attached to customer service has led to companies using computers to provide a faster and more responsive service. Customer phone enquiries are liable to be conducted by a 'help desk' viewing the customer's files on screen during the conversation. It is judged that attracting a new customer takes five times more effort than keeping an existing one. Furthermore, on average, a dissatisfied customer will tell 25 other people while a satisfied customer will tell just five others.

Telephones

The developments in telephone technology have played an important part in supporting the development of on-line computer communications. Telephones and the exchanges are likely to contain microprocessors and dedicated control circuitry allowing them to become more 'intelligent'.

The telephone handset may provide the facilities of an answering machine with incoming messages 'date stamped' so that on replay the listener knows when the message was left. The answering machine might also be capable of remote interrogation by sending a signal from any other phone. Depending upon the signal received the machine will replay the messages, erase the messages or rewind and reset the machine. Traditionally the messages are recorded onto tape but as RAM circuitry becomes more powerful and cheaper relatively short answer-phone messages can be recorded in RAM. This reduces the mechanical complexity of the device and also allows a smaller design.

Mobile phones are also having an impact on the use of telephones. The phone transmits and receives to and from local relay stations that form a network around the country. The use of digital signals ensures that there is no degradation of the signal. Unlike an analogue signal which, if degraded and then amplified, will then contain unwanted background 'noise' which cannot easily be separated out, a digital signal can be reconstituted as a perfect match of the original. This means that loss of strength between booster stations and the number of times a signal is boosted does not matter with digital signals and therefore distance is no object. This aspect is particularly important when computers are communicating over telephone systems.

Another significant development in communications technology is the use of fibre optics. The traditional method of passing electrical signals is through copper wire. The larger the diameter of the wire the less the loss of signal, thus in practice the choice of wire diameter is a compromise between diameter and bulk. The glass filaments of fibre optic cables have a significantly higher capacity than conventional wire cables thus fibre optic cables take up less space but can carry more information than equivalent wire cables.

A modem is needed to connect between a phone and a computer as described in chapter 1. This device might be in a separate unit but could equally be in the form of an add-on card that is inserted inside the computer's case. A modem card can be small enough to fit inside laptop computers or even personal organiser type computers. A personal organiser type computer used via a modem with a mobile phone provides a very portable way of connecting up to a computer network, independent of location and the availability of a power supply.

The plastic card

The credit card has been available for several years and the convenience of a plastic card of this size has led to the development of several other types of plastic cards. Cheque guarantee cards can also be used in bank ATM (automatic teller machine) machines, sometimes known as cash dispensers. Some banks have extended the use of this card so that it can be passed through an online device in stores and used to implement the transfer of funds direct from the account to the store's account. All these cards have magnetic strips on the reverse that carry encoded information relating to the holder and account.

Plastic cards with a magnetic strip are also used in some security systems. The holder has to swipe their card through a device at the entrance to gain admittance to the building or room.

Magnetic strip cards can also be used as prepayment cards. In some cases the card is purchased for a fixed fee, in other cases the card can be 'recharged' on further payment by passing it through a coin operated machine. Telephone cards are an example of fixed fee cards, the value of the cards being reduced during the duration of a telephone call. In some towns in the UK and Europe cards can be purchased to avoid carrying cash. The card is used in the local shops and its value is progressively reduced by purchases. Some claim the wider use of these cards will lead to the 'cashless society'.

An example of a rechargeable card is sometimes to be found in libraries where the prepayment card is used to obtain photocopies. The card might also double as a reader's card. However the checking out system used in many libraries is based upon the bar coded ISBN printed on the back cover of most books (see figure 8.1). If the library has standardised on bar coding for recording its transactions then the reader's plastic card is also likely to have their membership details in bar code form rather than magnetic strip.

ISBN 0-340-68349-X

9 780340 683491

Figure 8.1 An example of a bar code

Money and banking

Banking was one of the first commercial systems to use computerised input forms in dealing with customers, namely, the MICR (magnetic ink character recognition) characters pre-printed on to cheques. By pre-printing the cheque serial number, the bank branch sorting code and the customer's account number, only the cheque amount remains to be added.

MICR is particularly suitable for cheques because of the large amount of handling involved. All cheque transactions have to pass through clearing banks where they are sorted by branch codes allowing the cheques to be related to individual account numbers. To curtail some of the cheque handling involved, banks discourage customers from asking for their cheques to be returned with their bank statements. However, auditors and tax inspectors may require the production of the original cheque as evidence of payment, and so the practice cannot entirely be discontinued.

The advantage of using MICR, compared to OCR (optical character recognition) in this environment, is that MICR characters are not affected by marks made across them, whereas folds or marks can cause OCR documents to be misread.

Many cheques are paid in to a bank together with a pre-printed payment slip, for example, an electricity bill. The bill has account and payment details printed twice on it by computer. The customer keeps one part of the bill for reference, and the tear-off slip is returned to the electricity board's computer centre after payment, so that the customer's account can be updated. Hence, this type of bill is known as a turn-around document.

Bills contain much more variable information than a cheque, such as the customer's account number, name and address, and in the case of the electricity bill, the last and previous meter readings, electricity units consumed, price per unit and total amount to be paid. This information needs to be produced rapidly for millions of customers, making OCR the usual choice rather than MICR. The production of MICR documents requires special magnetic ink and greater accuracy, and is more costly.

In addition to processing individual cheques, the banks also have to process standing orders and direct debits for customers and to credit the customers' accounts with credit transfers, for example, when dealing with the payment of wages.

Banks may provide customers with plastic cards as previously described to enable then to obtain cash from cash machines situated inside and outside branches of the bank. When the card is put into the cash dispenser machine, the customer has to key in the identity number corresponding to the one held in the magnetic strip on the card. If the amount requested does not exceed the limit allowed and there is sufficient money in the account, the cash is dispensed in notes to the customer, and the balance in the account is debited automatically. Customers may also ask to see their bank balances on screen, request a statement or, on some machines, request the local printout of a mini statement showing the most recent transactions.

The advantages to be obtained from reducing the amount of cheque handling is leading banks to consider ways of directly debiting accounts by the use of on-line systems. This approach to banking is given the name electronic funds transfer (EFT). The most widespread us of EFT is likely to be in retailing, where by presenting a bank card, the customers will have their accounts debited immediately through an on-line system linking the store's point of sales terminal to the bank's computer.

Technology has reduced transaction costs and the need for a branch network. Branch networks are likely to become less important in the provision of financial services while postal and telephone banking increase in scale. As the entry barriers into banking have come down due to technology banks are facing increased competition. Banks are no longer the exclusive supplier of banking services. Many stores now offer credit cards and loan facilities. However banks are in a strong position to capitalise on their knowledge of customers. Some would say that banks are in the information business, for example, Barclays has the largest database of its kind in the world containing details of 15 million customers.

The current cost structures in banking are based upon the traditional branch-based network with heavy cross subsidies over the range of services offered. In future, the move will be towards more direct charging of specific services.

Perhaps the most significant development in the banking world over the past few years has been the development of telephone banking. Within 5 years a new telephone banking service built up 450,000 account customers and is attracting 10,000 new customers per month.

Banking has also become an activity without frontiers. A major British bank, part of an international group, offers a global banking service. Their electronic trading and risk management system operates 24 hours a day in more than 40 countries. Their ATM system allows card holders to use 170,000 machines in more than 70 countries worldwide.

Several banks offer a nationwide telephone banking service that allows customers to transfer funds, pay bills, and conduct most routine banking transactions 365 days of the year. They can be fully integrated with the branch network and do not require the customer to set up another account. The ATM network can include non-bank sites such as petrol stations, supermarkets and railway stations.

In addition, some banks have installed counter automation terminals through the branch network to allow faster processing of transactions. This provides the ability to clear cash on the same day and has speeded up the checking procedures as the information to be checked is on the cashier's screen. By displaying appropriate information onto branch computer screens the local staff are able to take decisions that would previously have had to be referred up the chain of command.

As lending becomes more competitive the need to only lend against good risks is important. Some banks allow customers to arrange loans over the phone. This is possible through the use of automated credit scoring systems and the analysis of customers' spending patterns. Loans to business customers are assessed by using a knowledge-based system as a lending advisor. These systems use a database to compare the company's financial performance with other companies in the same industry.

Retailing

Retailers initially used computers for accountancy applications, like any other business. A major advantage in having the accounts computerised is the closer control obtainable over creditors. Large-scale purchasing can also lead to substantial discounts, providing payments are made on time. A computerised system helps to ensure that these deadlines are met and not overlooked.

A retailing business is dependent on effective stock management, and therefore, as experience with computer systems grew, more attention was paid to monitoring the stock holding on a computer. Conventional accountancy systems allow the organisation to monitor the stock which has been brought into the company. Retailing, however, has special needs, in that stock goes out (i.e. is sold) in small quantities, and unlike manufacturing industry the stock movement is not pre-planned. There is therefore a special need to monitor details of the items sold, as accurately and as quickly as possible.

The development of cash tills has been with a view to the automatic recording of items sold. Initially, the conventional tally rolls in cash tills were replaced by ones which had transactions printed on them in OCR characters. This allowed the retained tally roll to be processed as input to a computer system at the end of the day or week.

As technology developed, alternative means of marking stock items became available; the most common being bar coding. To gain advantage from this, it is necessary to be able to capture the stock details at the time of the sale. The cash till therefore becomes a data entry device, whereby the information on the bar code can be read automatically by a wand or passed over a laser scanner. The information read may be combined with other details keyed in by the cashier and stored on a cassette tape or disk, or the information may be passed directly into a central computer system through a point of sale (POS) terminal.

The use of a POS terminal not only ensures that the computerised stock records are correctly maintained, but also speeds up significantly the feedback of information to management. Sales in a retail store are influenced by displays, special offers and regional differences in taste. On-line point of sales systems allow management to respond to what is happening now, as opposed to only being able to review the situation in retrospect. In large department stores, takings might be monitored hourly and action taken immediately to respond to problems of low takings and goods being out-of-stock.

An on-line system also allows management to monitor the general level of activity at specific POS terminals and to deploy sales staff more effectively. Some of the POS terminals can also read credit cards and hence reduce bad debts, for example, where the credit limit is being exceeded. In this case, the POS terminal will alert the finance office to send a manager, while a code on the POS terminal indicates to the sales assistant that the customer is to be detained until the problem is resolved.

In order to use POS terminals, stock items must be coded. In the case of large retailing groups, the codes may be those developed by the company. There are further benefits to be obtained, however, if the codes follow an agreed standard within the industry. An example of industry-wide standard coding is the use of bar coding within the food industry. This not only allows items pre-marked by the supplier to be read at any POS terminal accepting the bar codes, but also allows the supplier and vendor to exchange trading information with the minimum need for recoding to suit a particular computer system. As previously mentioned, the POS terminal might also have an electronic funds transfer capability to complete the sales side of the transaction.

Another area where the retailing industry has gained by the use of computer technology is in the use of hand held terminals by suppliers' representatives. During the day the representative keys details of the firm's orders into a hand-held data entry unit. At the end of the day, the unit is connected to a telephone in the representative's home or hotel and all the orders are transferred down the phone line to the supplier's computer. Sales representatives traditionally get involved in a great deal of paperwork which has to be sent to head office. Using a portable data entry unit reduces the paperwork and also reduces the order processing time, to the advantage of the purchasers.

Alternatively, information can be exchanged between representatives and their companies' offices by using a laptop computer and modem. This two-way communication has the advantage that representatives can find out the stock situation of various items and can receive messages. A company may also have its own private viewdata system linked to its data processing system, or it may use a bureau which specialises in this type of service.

Market research

A vast amount of market or survey research is carried out all over the world. Companies providing products or services need to know their customers' opinions about these, also what/how/when/why they are using the products/services, so that they can make improvements and increase their market share. Governments do research to find out information about their citizens so as to plan for the future. There are polls about political parties to compare voters' views on their performance and preferences. The surveys may be carried out by these organisations themselves or often by using research companies specialising in designing surveys and interpreting the results. There is a large amount of data to be processed and often the results are needed very quickly to be of value.

Let us see how computers are used throughout the process for designing and producing questionnaires, collecting and processing the results, for the final management reports and for further interrogation of the data. Using specialised software for each of these stages makes it easier and more efficient to achieve quick results. The first stage is to produce the questionnaire. This may need to be produced on paper for mailing out or putting into magazines, handed out in shops or at airports, etc.

Questionnaire design and production software has facilities for adding new questions and lists of possible answers (responses), retrieving questions from hard-disk archives, for cutting and pasting these into the new questionnaire and for producing a good quality desktop published version for printing.

Some questions will be pre-coded or closed questions. If only one choice is allowed from a list of responses, this is a single-coded response, or if more than one choice can be selected, it is termed multi-coded. Some answers will be in numeric form and some questions will be open end to allow a written answer to be given.

The questionnaire design package should have facilities for entering all these different types of questions and responses. Other special features available should include routing to a different part of the questionnaire according to the answer given, putting in codes against the responses to be used in the analysis, having different types of items such as rating scales, for example, a five-point scale from very poor to very good, and different types of responses as mentioned above.

An alternative to producing the questionnaire on paper is to produce an electronic version to be displayed on the computer's screen. This can be used with pen computers or multimedia notebook computers for Computer Assisted Personal Interviewing (CAPI), that is, face to face interviewing or for self completion.

Many surveys are conducted over the telephone. The interviewer will get a number to call from a database of selected numbers (the sample), dial the number to make contact, bring the questionnaire up on the screen and carry out the interview.

The sample may be based on quotas of people with certain attributes, for example, it may be required that a set number of males and females, in specific age ranges and occupations who live in particular areas, are to be interviewed. Once a quota has been reached, no more people with these characteristics will be interviewed. Using computers in this way is known as Computer Assisted Telephone Interviewing (CATI).

It is much more efficient if a computer can be used to dial the numbers and only give the call to the interviewer when a person has answered. This may be done by linking a telephone system to the CATI system so that the telephone computer selects numbers from the sample and dials them.

Such a system also allows music to be played over the telephone, for example, in questions related to recall of advertisements, to record answers to open end questions ('verbatims') and to avoid using interviewers for some applications by using digitised voice with responses keyed in by respondents from their touch-tone telephones.

Once the data is collected, it will need to be processed so as to produce tables of information and graphs; again using specialised software, geared towards the survey research industry, is the most efficient way of doing this. If the data has been collected by a CAPI or CATI system, it will already be in the correct format for processing. Paper questionnaires will need to be scanned into a computer or keyed in by hand.

Access can then be given to the data so that the end users – researchers, marketing managers, planners – can carry out further analysis on their PCs as required. The ability to explore the data for particular points of interest ensures that the maximum amount of information and value is gained from the survey.

Libraries

Libraries are basically information retrieval centres. Details of their stockholding (the catalogue) is held on a data base. In some cases this database may only contain the details of the specific library but in the case of branch libraries within a county the database will usually contain details of all the stockholding throughout the county.

The system of issuing books to readers usually involves scanning the reader's plastic bar coded ticket, scanning the bar coded details from the book and stamping the book with the return date. The reader's details and date due back are linked to the stockholding database. Subsequent enquiries of this database will show that the book is currently on loan and give the due date. Readers can access this information through terminals in the library, and in some cases, via the Internet or local county viewdata system. They cannot however access details of any current borrowers, unlike the library staff who have the security level to access details by the borrower's bar code number. Some systems allow an individual borrower to input their own bar code number to obtain a list of items currently on loan and their due date.

The on-line catalogue available to the reader usually has a series of menu-driven search facilities. Entering the details of a book's title or author will display the cataloguing details for the book. These would be the typical bibliographic information, i.e. author, title, publisher, year of publication and ISBN. In addition, the library's classification number and, if necessary, the branch location, together with its status (on shelf, on loan, reference, etc.) would be displayed. If more than one book meets the search criteria a numbered list of these books will be displayed. The fuller details of any one of these books is then obtained by entering the chosen number. If required it is possible to return to the list to view details of other books. When the list is long the screen can be scrolled or paged up and down to browse through the list.

The more elaborate catalogue searching systems will allow searches on words in the title and the use of wild cards for the title or author. In addition it may be possible to search by subject classification, either by entering the appropriate word, e.g. railways, or by entering the library's classification code. There is no one universal classification code used by libraries. Many public libraries use the Dewey classification scheme, the more academic libraries tend to use the American Library of Congress classification system, while specialised and in-company libraries might use their own system. The Dewey and American Library of Congress classification numbers are often printed by the publishers on the fly cover of the book to ensure libraries using these systems are consistent in their cataloguing of the book.

Sometimes, if the search is rather general, the list of books produced by a search can be very large. The search systems usually allow the user to narrow the range by combining words, e.g. railways AND Brunel, or by specifying date ranges, e.g. >1990 (meaning after 1990).

Several bibliographies and indexes that were traditionally available for consultation on microfiche are now available on CD ROM. Library services often now include facilities for accessing these CD ROM indexes and other multimedia CD ROM reference works such as ency-clopaedias.

School and home computers and computer games

Prices of computer equipment have fallen dramatically in recent years, and with the development of the low-cost microcomputer there has been a rapid expansion in computing in schools and at home.

Apart from games, home computers were initially mainly used for word processing with maybe some application of spreadsheets and databases and many households could not justify owning a computer. The advent of multimedia has led to many more computers being sold for home use.

A multimedia computer consists of a traditional personal computer but in addition has a sound card and speakers together with a CD ROM drive (see figure 8.2). The basic specification of the computer for multimedia also includes a high resolution colour monitor with video

Figure 8.2 A multimedia PC

circuits having their own dedicated memory. This allows fast changing screen displays to provide realistic animation. The software used in multimedia requires large amount of RAM so that it is not uncommon to have 16 MB of RAM with a hard disk capacity of 1 GB. CD ROM drives are available in difference data transfer rates. The basic speed is 150 KB per second but quad-speed (quadruple) drives, for example, can transfer data at the rate of 600 KB per second and drives can be obtained that exceed this transfer rate. Nevertheless this is still slower than hard disk transfer rates (around 2 to 3 MB per second) therefore reading directly from a CD ROM is slower than reading a hard disk. Therefore for some applications, such as games, it is better to have the software installed on a hard disk.

Schools tend to go for standard equipment recommended by educational authorities. The advantages of this are compatibility between different schools to allow exchange of software, and the availability of financial support for some of the equipment. In addition, many schools have purchased equipment through their PTAs (Parent–Teacher Associations). The ability to link to the Internet is seen as an important requirement in schools.

Computer applications in schools are varied and depend very much on the enthusiasm of the pupils and teachers. The use of the computer is integrated into many aspects of the curriculum and in addition the computer is used as a club activity.

Writing games software is a good educational exercise as it taxes the programmer's ingenuity, and involves reasoning and logic. Even using arcade-type games on a microcomputer can be educational, in that this can develop sensory and motor skills and may encourage students to start developing programs.

Just as computers in industry and commerce are used for data processing, the home or school computer can be used for simple record keeping associated with hobbies or project work. Files can be set up on disks and processed to produce lists, labels, and so on. Letters and reports can be produced using word processing.

Programming is time-consuming, and in many cases it is more important to use programs than to write them. A vast range of software is available on a commercial basis, and also from books, magazines, and through exchange schemes. Programs may also be obtained through the Internet.

The home computer market has developed out of the tremendous interest in computer games. As the number of games have increased, so has the justification for buying a home computer rather than a specialised games machine. The range of games is continually expanding, and can be compared to the pop music scene. Some software houses have achieved reputations for consistently good games and have a faithful following. One or two games have been so successful that they have been developed into a series with a consistent theme or character.

Early computer games were imitations of successful arcade games. Perhaps the first game to capture the public imagination and become well known was *Space Invaders*. This game is a typical invader game and is responsible for generating a whole range of similar games. At first, the home computer versions of the arcade games were cruder, but now there is little to choose between dedicated arcade machines and home computer versions of a game. The difference is largely due to economic factors rather than the compatibility of the microcomputer.

The features of arcade games are good graphics, fast action and realistic sound. These features are therefore expected in similar home computer games and are now largely met by the latest multimedia computers. More programming effort is required to develop high resolution displays, but as they become the norm, any arcade style game must incorporate them if it is to sell.

When playing a fast action game, it can be found that using a keyboard slows up the player's response. For this reason it is very common to use joysticks with an arcade style game. In addition to the computer manufacturer's authorised joystick, there are many designs of joystick available from specialist manufacturers. A responsive joystick makes all the difference between an average and a record score.

Because arcade games require a high degree of skill, there are several levels of play. The novice can start on the lowest level, and progressively work up to the higher levels as their skill increases. Some games have supplementary disks available that add on further levels. This also ensures that the game will retain its attraction for a long time, even for a quick learner. In addition to playing arcade games competitively with others, many people compete against themselves, trying to beat their best score to date. Most games therefore display the highest score in addition to the current score.

Space Invaders has been mentioned as an example of the early arcade game. The development of this style of game has given rise to a range of science fiction, space age shoot-out games. As the software market grows, the variations of arcade games continues to develop, but in all cases the emphasis is on fast action on the screen calling for quick responses from the player.

Another type of game that is in some ways more suited to computerisation is the adventure game. The traditional adventure game is played by a group of people, each having a collection of characters who undertake a joint expedition. The expedition can be set in a maze of dungeons or across unfamiliar lands. The objective of the game is usually to find treasure, and in their wanderings the expedition meets a range of fantasy creatures. The rules of the traditional adventure games are very open-ended, and usually an umpire (dungeon master) is used to plan the scenario, interpret the rules, and generally mastermind the game. The success of the game largely depends upon the management of the adventure by the umpire. However, it can take a long time for the umpire to interpret and arbitrate the game, and so the pace can be slow.

In many ways a home computer is ideal for adventure games. The computer, acting as umpire, is much quicker at making decisions. Also, you can play an adventure game on a computer by yourself, you do not have to arrange to meet with a group of friends. On the other hand, serious adventure gamers would argue that the interpersonal relationships of a joint expedition and the open-endedness of the rules made possible by using a human umpire are the most important features of an adventure. In simulating an adventure on a home computer, the game becomes very constrained by the programming logic. Thus a computer may at a certain stage only allow the player four courses of action, whereas a human umpire would consider any suggestion and judge it on its feasibility. The Internet has been used to overcome some of the limitations of computerising a game. On the Internet an adventure game can be played interactively with several players and there can still be a human adjudicator (dungeon master).

The success of a stand-alone computer adventure game is therefore dependent on the ingenuity of the programmer. Although they cannot replace the traditional adventure game, they do have advantages for the individual adventurer. Because of the in-built constraints, the computer adventure game becomes more of a puzzle solving game whereby the correct course of action needs to be found. Due to the limitations of a computer to accept free-style English, an instruction to the computer can be met with a standard 'I do not understand' response, for example, 'Pick up the mirror' may not be recognised, but 'Get mirror' may be accepted. A lot of time can be wasted trying alternative phrases which mean essentially the same thing.

Some adventure games are played solely with text messages and responses whereas others use graphics to display the situation. Text-based adventures can be more complex, but require the players to use their imagination. Younger players are more likely to prefer the graphic adventures. Adventure games can take many hours to complete, and so it is usual to have a 'save situation' facility, so that the game can be continued at a later date without having to start again from the beginning.

Variations of the adventure game can simulate a wide range of realistic situations. A common simulation, available for most microcomputers, is an aircraft flight simulation. Typically, you are required to land an aircraft using the instrumentation displayed on the screen. The more sophisticated of these games also show a 3-D view from the cockpit.

One type of gaming simulation, that had a large following before microcomputers became popular, and lends itself to computerisation, is war gaming. War games are run very much like adventure games, except that the scenario is based as closely as possible upon realistic situations. The comments made about adventure games largely apply to computerised war games, that is, they tend to be more restrictive than a traditional war game. An important, if not the most important, aspect of a war game is the management of your forces. Although a computerised war game is likely to provide you with a number of screen reports, it is still largely up to the player to organise the information available. This is a reflection of your competence as a commander and it is therefore up to you to decide what additional charts, maps, tables, and so on, are needed.

A range of traditional games are available on microcomputers. The attraction of playing these types of game on a computer is that you never lack an opponent, as you can play against the computer. In addition, if the games offer you levels of play, you can gradually build up your skill. The classic of traditional games, chess, is the most widely available. Other games such as backgammon, draughts, nim, othello, *Scrabble*, and several card games are also readily available.

One of the consequences of computerising these types of game is that the strategy of the game has had to be closely analysed. This means that with chess, for example, the standard of play by the computer has steadily increased as better algorithms, or programming rules, have been developed. Most microcomputers should be able to beat the average chess player when played at the highest level.

Chess games usually allow the player to choose their colour. Moves are entered via the keyboard using standard chess algebraic notation. Some chess programs contain a hint function which suggests the next move if required. Chess, however, is a complex game, and even with the speed of microcomputers the computer can take a long time to work out its next move. Depending upon the level of play, the computer's response may be anything from instantaneous to an hour or more.

Other features of chess games might include the ability to swop sides at any stage, and the means of saving a game. Swopping sides can be very instructive if you want to see how the computer would get you out of your currently hopeless position. Saving a game can be useful for the higher level, longer running game as you can play it over several days. The ability to replay a game in single steps is also useful for analysis. This feature is often linked to the ability to set up a position from a textbook and start from that stage.

Games such as backgammon are similarly highly developed, but word games such as *Scrabble* are harder to implement. This is because this type of game is very dependent on having an extensive dictionary in memory. The content of the dictionary not only determines the level at which the computer can play, but also which words it will recognise and accept from the player.

There are a variety of programs that, while not exactly games, may be used mainly for amusement. The type of programs in question are represented by astrology and biorhythm applications. The feature of these applications is that a large number of calculations are involved to produce the output. A home microcomputer is ideal for this purpose, so that a person interested in these areas can forget the technicalities and concentrate on the interpretation of the output.

Other types of program with a similar practical entertainment value are those that analyse your lifestyle, in response to a series of answers to questions, and state for example, that you should take more exercise.

The degree to which you treat these programs as pure entertainment depends on how seriously you regard the topic. If you are a serious believer in astrology, for example, then you would need to investigate the basis of the programming involved before accepting the output. The same applies to a health guide program or personality test.

9

DESIGN AND PLANNING

Introduction

Although most people are more aware of computers in retailing and commerce, the most marked effect of computers is in industry. The initial applications of computers led to 'islands of technology' but as the power of computers increased together with the development of networking standards the applications have become progressively integrated.

One of the first areas of industrial application was at the design stage using CAD (computer aided design) systems. Computer-based automation led to CAM (computer aided manufacture). As these two areas became linked the term CAD/CAM was used. Further integration of the design and manufacturing process then led to the term CIM (computer integrated manufacture).

The direct application of computers to the plant and equipment is termed process control. With the development of microelectronics, it has become possible to have individual items of plant controlled locally by their own computer (or microprocessor built into the equipment) with perhaps several such units under the general control of a central computer. An example of a stand-alone computer controlled machine is the CNC (computer numerically controlled) lathe. The machine can be programmed by the operator, as and when required, or it can read prepared instructions on punched paper tape or disk. Groups of these and similar machines can be grouped together into machining cells requiring only one operator per cell.

A FMS (flexible manufacturing system) is one or a group of computer-controlled machines coupled to a robotic part-handling system. The working area of a FMS is unmanned, the system being controlled remotely.

The spread of robotic applications is a particular example of this decentralised control. Prior to the development of microcomputers a robot would have a complex cable of wires connecting it to a large computer standing in the vicinity. The expense of such systems limited their economic application. Nowadays, with robots often costing less than a person, judged on normal investment criteria, it has become economic to construct complete factories operated by robots.

The modern manufacturing unit can demand a complexity of paper-work in its organisation and control. The application of computers can considerably simplify the problems of planning and control, thereby freeing the management to spend more time on planning and decision making.

Planning is at the heart of most commercial organisations. By its nature, planning requires that the company's general policies and strategy are followed through down to the minutest detail. The best decisions come from examining several alternatives. In practice, because of the detail involved, planning can be a time-consuming activity, and so there is often not the time to develop and examine alternative plans.

Management's problems are not over when the plans have been developed. Due to changing circumstances the plans may need to be revised, and once implemented, the data will need to be updated in line with progress.

The newer technologies have led to companies aiming for continuous improvement and hence there are always new projects being undertaken and change becomes the norm rather than the exception. As a consequence, project planning packages based upon CPA (critical path analysis) techniques are now common.

Using computers considerably aids planning and removes many of the above difficulties. It becomes possible for managers to ask and pursue many more 'what if ...' options, as the computer also speeds up and simplifies the updating of plans in line with actual progress achieved.

Management's control of production is often based around a MRP (materials requirements planning) system. The close control that a computerised system can maintain ensures that only the materials actually required are purchased or made. This helps to reduce unnecessary stock holding and work in progress.

——— Computer aided design ———

A large part of a designer's time can be spent in producing the drawings. The lines on the plans would have to be positioned accurately and side views, top views, and so on would also have to be projected from the original view. The computer can take over this time-consuming activity, and free the designers for the more creative aspects of their work.

The basic features of CAD packages are similar to other drawing packages. Straight lines, rectangles and circles can be created, enlarged, moved, copied or deleted as necessary. When several elements (lines) have to be built into a particular object, the elements can be designated as one group so any copying, re-scaling or moving is carried out on the object.

The software supplied with CAD systems allows the designer to sketch drawings or use functions for a more precise layout (for straight lines, arcs of circles, shading, and so on). The images can be rotated and translated to show the designer different views of the same object. Interactive controls allow zooming in and magnification to display an enlarged version of part of the design. Parts of drawings, for example, the windows in a house, may be stored and called up when required. The software library may include a number of standard shapes, such as symbols for circuit diagrams.

Scaling can be very important in CAD and the packages will make provision for working accurately to designated scales. CAD packages are usually vector based rather than bit mapped. With bit mapped systems individual screen pixels are turned on or off to mark the presence of a line. Expanding or contracting the image is then achieved by expanding or contracting the pattern of 'dots' and the computer cannot create finer detail. Vector based packages designate lines by reference to the co-ordinates that determine their shape and position. Re-scaling the lines causes the computer to display the lines as accurately as allowed by the screen resolution. Images can be easily tilted or rotated when the position of lines are held as co-ordinates as the computer can calculate the revised position of the end points of the line.

The more elaborate CAD systems allow the surfaces of a 'drawn' object to be shaded relative to a particular source of hypothetical illumination. The package may even allow the automatic generation of resulting shadows.

The above features allow a designer to draw an object and view it in three dimensions, rotating the object as required. These features impose a vast amount of calculations on the computer and powerful computers are required for this type of presentation. In some cases this level of detail is not required and 'wire-framed' models of the design might suffice. A 'wire-framed' model simply shows the face edges of the designed object, so that it may look like, for example, the wire-frame of a lampshade. A slight elaboration on the wire-frame option is to not show any of the lines that would be obscured from the current viewpoint.

In addition to these general types of drafting system, used basically for engineering drawing, software may be available for a particular CAD system that is aimed at more specific applications. For example, designers concerned with machines and their operations may require software that incorporates a model of a man and standard shapes that can be built into three-dimensional models of, say, people sitting at work stations or working in the home or a driver sitting in a vehicle.

The traditional design process can involve the engineers in a large amount of calculations. Often the calculations are iterative, that is, the calculation is done repeatedly, and each time the answer becomes more accurate. In practice, the cost of carrying out more than a few iterations would be prohibitive and so a less than ideal solution would be adopted. For example, a bridge would have to be designed deliberately too strong, to err on the safe side. A computer, by carrying out more iterations, can usually produce a design that meets the specification, but at the same time uses less materials.

Design engineers traditionally refer to a number of handbooks providing the vast number of formulae that form the basis of much of the design task. This type of information is now available on CD ROM so that not only can the CD ROM be searched for particular calculations but, when retrieved, the formulae can be used interactively on screen to solve the equations.

Another type of CAD software system may incorporate project information. Software is required for manipulating the design, performing stress calculations, and controlling the ordering of materials and project phases. A database is built up as the project progresses, containing details of components, items of equipment and layouts. The latter can be displayed on the screen, manipulated, and stored as updated versions in the database. Various checks can be incorporated according to rules specified by the engineers and clashes with these identified. Another advantage is the availability of up to date information, stored in the database, to all the engineers working on the project, thus ensuring consistency in the various parts of the design.

For example, CAD techniques are used extensively in the design of microchips (integrated circuits). A microchip may consist of many layers of semiconductor material, such as silicon, separated by insulating layers of, say, silicon dioxide. Each layer has its circuit pattern engraved on it, and this is etched into the insulating material by a masking process known as photolithography.

The next stage after design in some industries is the building of a prototype model in wood or clay to enable a better appreciation of the appearance of the design in three dimensions. It is also a useful aid in discussing the product's manufacturability, the suitability of the styling, etc. Rapid prototyping is a term used for the automatic manufacture of a prototype from the CAD information. The ability of a CAD system to analysis the design as a series of thin slices or layers allows this information to be used in a process to build up the model layer by layer in coatings of resin. The ease and speed (days) of producing prototypes this way reduces the development time from weeks to days and also makes design changes more economic.

It is often desirable to experiment with the design of new systems or products. Many aspects of this experimentation can be carried out on a computer in simulations. Computer simulation may also be used to train new employees, as in the case of the drilling operations of oil rigs. If the trainee makes a mistake on a computer model, little harm is done. In addition a computer can simulate proposed administrative changes, to aid management in determining the best policies to adopt.

When engineers design a complete plant in a process industry, such as a nuclear reactor plant, they have to consider where to locate many items of equipment and the layout of the necessary services, such as ducting for electric cables. In these types of application the use of virtual reality systems can be a considerable help.

Virtual reality

The increasing power of computers and the speed of updating or 'refreshing' screens have allowed the CAD concepts of displaying an object in three dimensions, moving and rotating it, to be applied to more than one object. The screen can display an environment of several objects and the view point can be that of someone situated within the environment. A virtual office for example can be displayed and one can move around it. The results of moving the furniture are immediately apparent.

The original form of virtual reality, termed the 'immersion' technique requires one to wear a helmet to see the environment (see figure 9.1). The helmet incorporates a small LCD screen in front of each eye which displays a continuous updated view of the virtual world. Head movements are detected by magnetic sensors and the virtual scene moves accordingly. Further interaction is possible by the use of gloves which monitor hand movement, allowing virtual objects to be grasped or picked up. The disadvantage of using headsets are that they need recalibrating between users and after about 30 minutes use the user tends to suffer from a form of motion sickness.

The other approach to viewing virtual reality is termed 'interactive visualisation'. The virtual environment is displayed on a screen and a

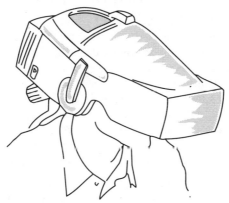

Figure 9.1 A virtual reality headset

mouse is used to 'fly' through the environment. The screen is usually the normal computer's monitor screen but some companies have built virtual reality theatres where one is surrounded by a 180-degree curved screen. The screen comprises several aligned projections from monitors. The advantages of desktop virtual reality are the lower cost, faster screen updates and better definition, and the ability to display the environment on several monitors for multiple viewing presentations.

Virtual reality systems were first developed in the 1970s by the military to improve the pilots' flying ability and are now also used, for example, for tank simulation exercises. They are now used on a wider scale in a number of industries. The ability to 'walk' through a building and view it from different angles has been applied during the design of buildings by architects. It has also been used in the design of process plants where there are problems in fitting in all the plant's pipework and cabling and dealing with any clashes. Supermarkets have also used virtual reality to assess various store layouts and the presentation of goods. A manufacturer of household appliances has created a virtual reality kitchen that allows any of its products to be seen *in situ*.

Manufacturing systems

A manufacturing system can involve a mass of paperwork. The traditional works order system would include the paperwork issued and monitored by the Production Control Department as described below.

On receipt of an order, the Production Control Department would create materials requisition slips that authorised the issue of sufficient materials from the stores. To do this they would have to consult parts lists, which contained details of what had to be produced to meet the order. Having identified individual parts that needed manufacturing, the Production Control Department would then have to consult the process planning documentation. This would tell them how much material to issue per item (taking into account a specified wastage rate), and would also give details of each stage of the production process, that is, the sequence of machines to be used, the time allowed per operation, and any inspection stages required.

When the above procedure is done manually, it results in a set of documents being produced for each order. This often meant that in order to clear it, the paperwork was issued as fast as it was raised. The effect of this was that work was started unnecessarily soon and, due to congestion, one job would delay another. In these circumstances the company would employ a team of progress chasers to expedite the jobs that were late.

The typical manual production control system resulted in high work-in-progress and late deliveries. Computerisation was first applied, in the days of punched cards, to separating the original orders into their component parts, and producing the documentation for, typically, a week ahead. Thus computer updating runs would be done at the end of the week to provide an up-to-date work load for the start of the following week.

These production control systems helped reduce inventories and provided up-to-date reports of progress to management, but weekly control was still crude, as the actual situation was liable to change hourly. With the development of on-line systems, control was improved as the progressing and reporting periods shortened. However, there was one major factor that was not taken into account by these systems, namely the capacity of the individual processes. This would have increased the amount of information to be interrelated and processed beyond the capabilities of the computer systems. This has now changed with the availability of databases. The production control systems nowadays have almost an unlimited scope to interrelate data and this has given rise to systems which have at their heart a capacity requirements planning and a materials requirements planning (MRP) module.

The modern system starts with a proposed sales program made up of firm orders and forecast orders. The implications of this are assessed by having the computer break down the orders into their required work-load on machine centres and compare this to the centre's current capacity. The sales program is only finalised when it can be seen that it is feasible in the light of the current work-load and available capacity. As a result of this stage, the need to sub-contract or work overtime and the cost implications, can be examined in advance.

The materials requirements planning stage works backwards from the required delivery date, to determine when materials must be issued. In this way, work is not started before it is necessary, and therefore work-in-progress is reduced. Because the materials requirements planning stage works right back to indicate when the raw material is required to be issued from stock, stock levels can be held at a minimum. Stock is bought in against a firm plan, not on the basis of topping up the shelves.

As the capacity of computer systems increases, the production control system can be integrated further with the order processing and accounts system to improve cash flow, with the distribution system to improve vehicle routing, and with costing systems to improve management control.

Simulation

Simulation is used in industry in two broad areas, to train people and to test out alternative ideas or designs before making a decision. A flight simulator is an example of simulation methods being used to train pilots, while a simulation of lorries loading and unloading at a warehouse is an example of how the number of loading bays might be decided. Before discussing examples of simulation, a brief explanation of the principles will be given.

Everyone has probably been involved in a simulation although they may not have realised it. Many board games, such as *Monopoly*, are simulations. In *Monopoly*, the buying and development of property is simulated, and the winning of a prize is determined by drawing the appropriate card from the pack. In business simulations, the chance of an event occurring is represented more accurately, so that the consequences are more realistic, but there is less need for a physical model, such as the miniature houses in *Monopoly*.

Many board games make use of dice to determine the move, for example, the need to throw a double six to get out of jail. In this case, the chance of getting out of jail is one thirty-sixth because there are thirty-six possible results from two dice. Some games, such as TSR Hobbies' *Dungeons and Dragons*, make use of more unconventional dice with eight, or twenty sides, etc. to simulate the odds required by the rules. In industrial simulations, a computer can be used to select random numbers, as though a die had been thrown. Unlike using a conventional die, the computer is not restricted to selecting numbers between one and six. The instructions in the simulation program enable a computer to choose a number at random over any specified range. Thus if there is a one in ninety chance that a lorry will break down, the computer can, in effect throw a ninety sided die to determine whether the lorry breaks down. When a simulated breakdown occurs, the computer can continue and select a further number at random to determine if the breakdown is due to a flat tyre, or some other reason. Quite complex situations can be simulated in this manner, the program sometimes being referred to as a simulation model.

The purpose of having a simulation model is to allow changes to be made in the model rather than in the real situation. In this way, alternative ideas can be tried out without making expensive mistakes or causing accidents in the real situation. Students of chemistry and scientists studying industrial processes, experiment with a computer model so that if the simulated equipment blows up no harm is done. Even when the changes could safely be made in the real situation, it may be quicker to use a simulation model. One year's operation of a stock control policy may be simulated within minutes on a computer so that the management do not have to wait a year to find out the consequences of a proposed change.

The most common situations to simulate are problems of flow that might give rise to queues. In practice, the rate of flow is seldom uniform and the slight variability can cause queues. Examples of this are road traffic, particularly at junctions, customers in banks, launderettes, etc. Industrial applications may be concerned with modelling the flow of work through the plant. The study of queues and bottlenecks allows design decisions to be made in relation to the number of duplicate items of plant needed, the space required for the work in progress (i.e. the queue), etc.

As an example of simulation, consider the following situation. A maintenance department has been maintaining an electric heat treatment oven for some years on the basis of changing elements as and when they fail. The Production Manager is now complaining that with the current work load he cannot afford so much downtime.

When a single element is replaced it takes six days, including the cooling-down and re-heating time. The Production Manager argues that if one element has failed then the rest must be near the end of their lives and it would make better sense to change the whole lot, particularly as changing all six elements would not take six times as long, but only twelve days, that is, twice as long. The accountant, while seeing that the Production Manager's idea would increase the time the oven was available, is worried about the extra money that would be spent on replacement elements.

The above situation could be resolved by trying out the Production Manager's suggestion for a while and keeping records of the effect, but it could prove an expensive mistake. Alternatively, the situation could be simulated on a computer as follows.

An examination of past maintenance records would give details of the element breakdowns. If these were consolidated into a single chart, it would be possible to establish the chance of any element lasting, for example, 30 days, 35 days, and so on. From this data the situation inside a hypothetical oven can now be simulated. The computer can generate a random number proportionate to the life of an element. If this is repeated six times, then the computer can set up in its memory an oven which contains six typical elements.

The next steps depend upon which maintenance policy is being simulated. Let us simulate the original policy, changing elements as and when they fail. As the computer knows the lives of all the elements, it can identify which element will fail first. The life of this element determines the oven's running time. This element can be replaced by a new one in the computer's memory by programming the computer under these conditions to select a new element at random. Finally, the computer can subtract the running time from the lives of all the other elements to determine their remaining lives.

By repeating the above procedure several times, the computer can simulate the running and breakdown of the oven over a long period. When several thousand breakdowns have been simulated the computer can cost out the consequences of this policy.

Slight modifications of the program would allow the computer to simulate any other maintenance policies that were suggested. In this way, only better ideas would be implemented and costly mistakes would be avoided.

Critical path planning

In addition to using the computer to carry out financial analyses, the computer can be used in the subsequent planning of any decisions implemented. Figure 9.2 shows a simplified plan, for the launch of a product, as a network. Each activity, such as print packaging, is shown as a box. The network diagram shows that this activity can only follow the design packaging activity and must precede the package first batch activity. A network chart that uses this convention is called a precedence diagram. The diagram also shows that, for reference purposes, this activity has been assigned the number 40 and it will take three weeks.

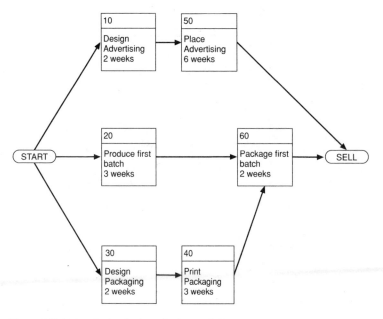

Figure 9.2 Network plan for launch of a product

The information contained in figure 9.2 is the data required by a project management package. From an analysis of this data, the computer produces a schedule as shown in figure 9.3. In this simple case it is possible to calculate manually that the project will have to take 8 weeks, due to activities 10 and 50. This means that there are 3 weeks to spare in the sequence 20–60 and 1 week to spare in the sequence 30–40–60. As the sequence 10–50 determines the duration of the project this path through the network is termed the critical path. Heavily shaded bars indicate that these two activities must be completed in the planned time period. The lightly shaded bars indicates the time periods scheduled for the other activities, and the extent by which these schedules can slip without extending the total project period of eight weeks is shown by continuation lines. Most commercial packages are capable of producing these schedules as well drafted bar charts. On colour printers the critical path would most likely be printed in red.

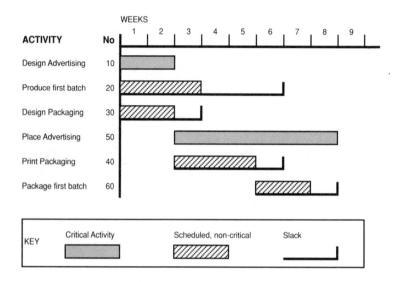

Figure 9.3 A critical path schedule

In practice, with a project consisting of perhaps 500 activities, it becomes very laborious to identify the critical path and develop a schedule without a computer. A project management package can not only do this but it will total the precise resources required, period by period and also calculate the cumulative planned cost.

The use of the package does not stop at the project planning stage. During the implementation of the project it is important to be able to calculate the effects of delays. A project management package can easily recalculate the critical path and develop revised schedules as the project progresses.

Project management packages are invaluable for planning and controlling the launch of new products, the maintenance and overhaul of plant, the construction and layout of new premises, etc. In fact the more technology brings about the need to change the greater the scope for project management packages in planning and controlling the changes required.

10

COMPUTER MONITORING AND CONTROL

The heart of a computer is the microprocessor. The traditional desktop computer represents a particular configuration suitable for more general purpose input, storage and output. In dedicated control situations, e.g. washing machines or sewing machines, the user is only aware of the controls provided by the designers. However, microprocessors are present in many everyday items to monitor and control their operation. For example, washing machines might contain three microprocessors, TV sets contain up to five and a BMW has more computers than a Saturn rocket according to one newspaper report.

Computers are essentially machines that use digital techniques based upon high/low voltage signals and circuits in an on/off state. Input and output ports from a computer can therefore be very conveniently used to monitor or initiate switching action. Switching action is the basis of many control situations. For example a motor may be activated by the computer to move an arm until the arm's position closes a microswitch. The switching action is fed back to the computer so that it knows the arm is in place and it can proceed to some other actions determined by the program it is following. The circuits for the motor and external microswitches however need to be isolated from the computer's because the current flowing in computer circuits is quite low but the current required to power motors and similar devices can be much greater. The isolation is achieved by using relays in the same way that an ignition switch in a car is isolated from the starter motor by a solenoid (starter relay). The current required by a starter motor would destroy an ignition switch. When the ignition switch is turned, the low current closes a relay which connects the starter motor direct to the car battery. Specific interface devices based on relays may be built but general purpose interface modules are available for connecting to either the parallel printer port, the serial port or as an interface card. Control of the pin connections can usually be achieved in most scientific-based languages such as BASIC or C.

Another type of interface is required when analogue signals are to be generated or to be monitored. Analogue signals are ones where the voltage (or possibly current) varies in proportion to the signal being monitored. This works in a similar way to a traditional clock, for example, which is an analogue device where the hands move round the dial in proportion to the passage of time. A digital clock on the other hand, displays time directly as numbers. A temperature probe's resistivity, for example, may vary with temperature. Circuitry connected to the resistive load can then output a voltage that varies with temperature. A circuit to convert this analogue signal to a digital one is termed an A/D converter. Similarly a unit that converts a digital signal (usually from the computer) to analogue form is termed a D/A converter.

Transducers are devices that can convert a non-electrical variable into electric signals, or vice versa. Transducers, in the form of sensors, can be used to monitor speed, temperature, weight, and so on, and pass this information back to a computer system. The computer can issue instructions in the form of electrical signals which, when passed to transducers designed as actuators, will stop a motor, close a valve, move a linkage, and so on.

Process control

The natural extension of using computers to control the organisational and administrative aspects of production is to use computers to control the plant and equipment. Over the years many items of plant and processes have been made more automatic, but computers allow far greater integration and control of the total process.

An example of process control might be found in an agricultural animal feed mill. One typical mill produces about 80 different animal feedstuffs, with up to 20 ingredients per mix. A controlled quantity of raw material can be discharged as required from the appropriate hopper, and either directed into a mill (a machine to grind the raw material down to a specified particle size), or sent directly to a hopper which feeds the mixer. Output from the mixer is passed to another hopper, from where the mix is routed according to the bagging required.

Several times a week the mill will be offered raw materials at prices that sometimes can only be held for one or two hours. As the cost of the raw materials varies, it is necessary to vary the ingredients in a mix to minimise costs while maintaining the nutritional balance. A computer is used to develop the least-cost formulations, which can be accessed by the commercial director. The formulations developed by this computer are passed to another computer that controls the mill. The mill computer, in turn, passes details of stock used back to the commercial computer.

The principles of process control can be applied in many industries, for example, mining, cement, chemicals and paper-making. In each case, the control system needs to be developed around the basic industrial technology that is used. Thus in mining, the monitoring and positioning of the cutting heads and the monitoring of environmental conditions are examples of the issues involved. In the cement industry, the monitoring of particle sizes and control of furnace temperatures are important. To achieve economies of scale in the production of chemicals, for example ammonia and ethylene, very large plants have been developed. The cost of a malfunction is prohibitive, and there is a need to reduce pollution and the use of energy as much as possible. All these requirements lead to an increase in the sophistication, and a greater degree of process control. The use of computers allows as much integration of the industrial process as required. The limitations are largely in understanding the process and the economics of implementing control procedures. One everyday example of process control is given by the engine management system fitted to many cars.

—— Engine management systems ——

The design and setting of controls during the operation of an engine require the optimal balance of conflicting specifications, i.e. low fuel consumption versus good acceleration. Applying microcomputers to the job of monitoring current conditions and altering engine controls, as is done in engine management systems, is a specific case of process control. One engine management system monitors the following seven parameters: barometric pressure, carburettor air temperature, coolant temperature, crankshaft position, exhaust gas recirculation (EGR) valve position, manifold pressure, throttle position. Signals from these sensors are sent to the control unit which computes three parameters: correct ignition timing, EGR flow rate and airflow rate, and sends the appropriate commands to adjust the ignition unit, EGR solenoid and airflow solenoid, at about 20 times a second.

Robots

Robots are used in industry for a variety of tasks which are repetitive and easily programmed. Some industrial robots are designed to move around the factory floor in a limited way, but most remain fixed in one place.

A typical robot used in a manufacturing environment has a single arm that can move in three planes over a wide work-area. Different hands may be inserted at the wrist end of the arm, for gripping different objects or for scooping up powders and liquids.

The hand may also be a tool for drilling, welding or spraying, or an electromagnet for picking up and dropping objects. Thin materials can be handled by using vacuum cups made of an elastic material. The vacuum seals can grip tightly without damaging the material, which is released quickly when the vacuum is broken.

In many industrial situations, robots are fitted with devices which enable them to select and move objects. These devices may be sensors which detect physical contact with objects (pressure-sensitive devices) or which respond to changes in a light beam (photoelectric devices) so that transparent and opaque objects can be distinguished. Inductive sensors can distinguish between objects having different magnetic properties, such as brass and steel.

Signals from sensors are fed back to a computer for processing. The computer can then send a signal to the robot to cause it to move its arm and hand to grip the workpiece and lift it to the correct position, using electric and hydraulic power if necessary. Computers and various memories are available as single microchips, so that the computer controlling the robot's action is small enough to be placed inside the robot.

Programming of robots may be carried out by people who understand the actions required but lack extensive programming expertise, by using special robot languages. Another way to teach the robot is by physically moving it through the required cycle in 'learning mode'. During 'learning mode' the robot's movements are recorded as data so that they can be subsequently read by a control program enabling the robot to repeat the cycle of movements over and over again.

It is possible to have automated factories controlled by robots under the supervision of one or two human operators, whose jobs may involve starting and setting up machines, and dealing with breakdowns. Using robots has a number of advantages, for example, whereas human operators need rest periods and can only work for limited shifts, robots can continue to work indefinitely, apart from non-productive periods (down time) due to breakdowns or routine maintenance.

Robots are not only used in the work-place to carry out tasks such as welding or paint spraying but, in the form of AGVs (autonomous guided vehicles), they are used to handle, move and store materials. The vehicles contain microprocessors that control their actions but also rely on tracks for guidance. These can simply be lines painted on the floor detected by light sensitive cells at the front of the vehicle. In a dirty environment the vehicle may track a cable laid beneath the surface by detecting the electromagnetic radiation from high frequency signals passing through the cable. Other sensors on the vehicle can pick up marks placed along the track allowing the vehicle to follow particular branches and loops as required. For safety, obstacle detectors are also incorporated into the vehicle so that it should not collide with other vehicles, or people.

Equipment in automated warehouses can stack and place pallets of goods in very confined spaces. The movements of the pallets are controlled by a computer either from an operator using a control panel or by automatically reading product codes as a pallet passes a detection unit. The product code is then converted into information representing the co-ordinates of the required storage position.

Compact car-parking units are based upon similar principles. A car to be parked can be raised through ten levels and positioned either to the right of left of the central lifting shaft. Before the car is moved around lasers scan the registration number and also check that no doors are open. When the car owner leaves the car to be parked they are issued a magnetic ticket that on re-presentation allows the automatic ramp to retrieve the right vehicle.

Human operators can work only in conditions that are not too hot or too cold, with sufficient space to move comfortably and with enough air and light. There are minimum working conditions which employers must provide for their employees. Robots, on the other hand, can be designed to work in extreme conditions, for example, in a narrow space and in a poisonous atmosphere.

Research into artificial intelligence (AI) is leading to the design of more intelligent robots so that the signals coming in from sensors can be interpreted in a more human way. For example, a human operator can observe if something is going wrong, and quickly take corrective action. A robot has to be programmed to detect abnormal situations through its sensors, and the corrective action may be to shut the machine down or to send a warning message to the factory supervisor.

The main limitations of robots are in their ability to see and in the intelligence that can be provided through computer programs. Investigations into stereo imaging techniques, using video cameras and optical pattern recognition, will lead to robots being able to select an object from a bin containing different industrial parts and orient it correctly for machining and assembly.

Vision systems can be based simply upon the use of a conventional television camera whereby the analogue signals are digitised via an interface into a pattern of binary 1s and 0s. A better alternative is to use a digital camera based upon a charge-coupled device (CCD). A CCD is an array of light sensitive cells integrated into a chip. The visual image is optically focused onto the surface of the CCDs to produce directly the electronic pattern of 1s and 0s. A system that classifies an image into areas of just black and white is a two grey level system. More elaborate classification of the image can give up to 256 different grey levels. To capture a picture in colour requires 24 bits of data per picture element which might have a resolution of 756 by 504. Data compression techniques are then used to reduce the image storage's requirement to, say, approximately 32 KB. High compression techniques lead to loss of picture quality so in practice there is a trade off between storage requirement and picture quality. Some cameras allow the user to choose the level of quality.

A robot with a vision system might be taught to recognise objects by the application of neural networks. Neural networks are based upon how our brain, constructed from a network of millions of neurons, is thought to work. A neural network is constructed from collection of RAM chips. Points on the visual image are connected at random to the RAMs, which in learn mode generate a pattern of 0s and 1s from the RAMs. When an image is viewed the same random points are assessed and a score calculated from the number of points that match the learnt pattern. Thus if a photo of a particular face was learnt and the same face together with two others were then assessed by the vision system the original face might score an 80% match while the other faces only score 50%, if slightly similar and 10% if completely different.

——— Automatic measurement ———

The ability to measure dimensions accurately is fundamental to science and engineering and the manufacture of high precision products. The developments in computer processing power and interfacing techniques have had a significant impact on measurement techniques both in terms of 'capturing' the measurements and the data analysis.

Many companies requiring a general purpose high precision measuring device use a co-ordinate measuring machine (CMM), see figure 10.1. A CMM has a probe that can move in three dimensions over a precision flat bed. The movement is achieved by a gantry that moves forwards and back (one axis of movement) with a cross slide (the second axis of movement) that carries a vertical column (the third axis) on which a probe is mounted. The precise position of the probe can be described by its position along the three axes (x, y and z). The probe ends in a 'perfectly' spherical tip which is sprung loaded to trigger a measurement at a predetermined pressure. If a diameter is to be accurately measured the probe is moved via joy stick controls against the article in, say, six different positions around the diameter. In each case when the predetermined probe pressure is reached the x,y,z co-ordinates are captured into a computer. Having obtained six sets of co-ordinates the computer software calculates the statistical 'best fit' circle to obtain the diameter of the article.

The computer software can not only calculate distances and diame-

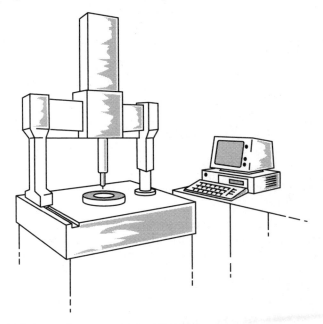

Figure 10.1 A co-ordinate measurement machine

ters based upon co-ordinate readings, it allows a CMM operator to program the movement of the probe so that in repetitive situations the CMM can automatically go through a cycle of measurements. Because all the measurements are based on calculation of co-ordinates relative to each other the work piece being measured does not have to be positioned accurately on the measurement bed.

Hand measurement gauges such as micrometer and vernier gauges are also available with a computer serial port. This port allows the current measurement to be passed directly into a computer-based system so that data can be captured directly for analysis.

Measurement data captured from CMMs or hand gauges are often the basis of a statistical process control (SPC) system. An SPC system monitors the variation from one measurement to another and relates the variation to statistically based control limits. If the reading is within the limits then the reading is acceptable. If the reading is outside the limits then this is regarded as such a statistically unlikely event that an investigation is required. In practice, under these circumstances the process would be stopped and the cause of the variation sought. Typical causes would be that the cutting tool had chipped, the work being cut has moved in the clamps, etc. An SPC system usually requires that a suspect measurement from a gauge is re-measured as it is important to validate the data reading before acting on the resulting analysis.

Satellites

The development of satellite technology has had an impact on a number of application areas, notably weather forecasting and terrestrial location systems.

Meterological offices round the world monitor and exchange information from a number of satellites, for example, America has weather satellites monitoring America and the Pacific area, India, the Indian Ocean, etc. These satellites are effectively in a stationary orbit relative to the earth and can scan a sector of the globe. Their angle of view however is not suitable for the polar regions and additional satellites are used specifically for these areas. Various views and features of the earth can be obtained according to the wavelength monitored. The actual weather forecasts are produced by elaborate computer weather models and even so the forecasts issued by the metrological offices are an interpretation from these models. The major advantage of satellite weather monitoring is the ability to obtain an overview of the dynamics of the changing weather patterns.

Wind speeds at sea level are deduced from microwave scatter meters that measure the roughness of the surface of the sea. The proportion of signals that bounces back from the sea's surface depends upon the sea's waves (which are whipped up by the wind). Improved forecasts come about through a greater number of readings (compared to relying on ships to pass on information) and better computer modelling. Using a satellite results in 15 times more information in the northern hemisphere and 100 times more in the southern (there is less shipping in the southern hemisphere). The direction of the wind is deduced from a computer model.

The existence of satellites allows their signals to be used as the basis of land-based positioning system. The satellite based Global Positioning System (GPS) is controlled by the US Department of Defense. The system uses 24 satellites circling the earth at 20,000 km with orbit times of 12 hours. The simultaneous reception of signals from four or more satellites can be used to calculate absolute position and height above sea level (see figure 10.2). The small size of integrated circuits allow the required receiver circuitry and processor to be built into a hand-held 'compass'. Such a compass is far more sophisticated than a normal magnetic compass. Its LED display can give a position to within 100 metres. This accuracy can be increased to 10 metres if the position from the satellites is compared to a known position and the error used as a correction. There is a choice of different co-ordinate systems to display a position according to the map being used. The memory allows up to 1000 positions to be stored together with a seven-character name. The compass can display the bearing and distance from its current position to any of these. The LCD also shows a directional arrow pointing to the required destination.

Figure 10.2 Global Positioning Satellites

A similar approach is available for tracking cars and car rescue services. A device in the car can determine its position from the GPS network and this information can then be transmitted over a mobile phone system to land-based emergency services. Even if the driver is lost the emergency service will know the location.

The sophistication and high hourly cost of operating aircraft make them a natural user of microcomputer systems. Large aircraft can obtain benefits from a distributed processing approach, that is instead of one central on-board computer, dedicated microcomputer systems can be assigned to each control system and interconnected. Apart from any operating efficiencies, the saving in cable runs (and hence weight) can justify this approach.

Small aircraft having smaller crews can obtain many benefits from the analysing capability of a microprocessor-based navigation system. The extreme example of this being single-seater fighter aircraft.

Commercial airlines can utilise microcomputer systems in many facets of their operations. Two are described here: passenger handling, and flight management.

Passenger handling

One major airline is using microcomputers to control the embarkation of airline passengers through turnstiles for internal flights. At the check-in gate a boarding pass is produced by a special printer. The boarding pass is printed with details of the journey in 'plain language' for the passenger and also in encoded information which can be read automatically by the barriers at the gate lounge.

A computer maintains a record of the number of boarding passes issued and provides a constant picture of information relating to passenger flow as it actually happens, i.e. in 'real-time'.

It is intended to extend the passenger system further by introducing credit cards that can be used in a similar manner to cash point machines to issue passengers with their tickets. Previously the airline's passengers completed a boarding card in the departure lounge. When the flight was called, those who arrived at the plane first obtained seats. This system caused confusion and rushes to the plane. In some cases, passengers did not obtain seats even though they had arrived early in the departure lounge. The new system gives passengers their own individual flight numbers. When the plane is to depart only the relevant numbers are called. The 'ticket' acts as a seat reservation system. On internal flights, the passenger pays on the aircraft. Previously, the passengers bought their tickets prior to entering the departure lounge. Although the control of passengers will be smoother, some passengers may not like the loss of a more personal system.

Flight management

Microcomputer-aided flight management can make substantial improvements to fuel economy. Normally, fuel economy is dependent upon the attentiveness of the flight crew and their ability to determine an optimum flight path. For example, starting the engines one minute later prior to taxiing would save tens of thousands of pounds per year on a major aircraft fleet. Similar savings can be made by reducing the taxiing time. Operating within a small margin of optimum altitude can save trip fuel; this can amount to several million pounds a year for major airlines. Cruising marginally faster than optimum uses more fuel. If the aircraft is retrimmed in flight to compensate for changes in the centre of gravity further fuel savings are made. Several million pounds may be wasted through inappropriate descent rates. To assist in these and other aspects of flight management, several airlines are using a performance data computer system.

This type of system interfaces with sensors which measure atmospheric conditions and aircraft characteristics and computes the optimum flight profile for best operating costs. There are four sensor inputs: temperature of outside air, altitude, air speed, fuel weight. The pilot inputs 'dispatch data' into the computer prior to take off. This information includes outside air temperature, height above sea level of airport at destination, quantity of reserve fuel and fuel for nearest alternative airport, weight of aircraft (including payload less fuel), a given index indicating relationship between fuel cost and time cost.

Once the dispatch data has been entered, the crew can, during the preflight phase, assess the effect of changing the flight plan received. This may be necessary and/or worthwhile because flight plans are based upon meteorological information and traffic conditions that are perhaps four hours old. The severest operational use of aircraft engines occurs during takeoff. This use of the engines, although of only a short duration, is the single largest contributor to the degradation of the engine performance. The computer system provides for three modes of operation and appropriate parameters can be selected and engaged by the pilot.

During climb the crew traditionally have a choice of two schedules – fast or slow. With the flight management system four modes are offered: economy climb, maximum rate, constant rate, and a thrust target. In each case, with the sensors monitoring the prevailing conditions the optimum climb profile is followed. During the flight, whenever the altitude departs from the optimum, this fact is displayed to the crew. Predictions of current range, in distance and time, are displayed. The crew can enter alternative wind speeds, etc. and be given predictions of the effects of these changes. This type of information, which can be required very rapidly if an engine has to be shut down, can also be analysed further by the flight management system to indicate alternative modes of operation to achieve, for example, greatest cruising range under an 'engine out' condition. Failures within the airborne computer system itself will be stored in memory to be interrogated by the maintenance force on landing but in addition, some ground maintenance sites are equipped to receive details of malfunctions while the aircraft is in flight and before it has landed. This allows the maintenance staff to diagnose and prepare for the maintenance required thereby reducing turn-round time.

--------------------- **Medical** ---------------------

The use of computers in medicine are similar to their use in business, administration and in industry. The develop of computer networks aids the exchange of administrative information and possibilities for remote consultations while the developments in sensor and monitoring devices have increased the sophistication of diagnostic and treatment possibilities.

There are many administrative advantages from networking surgeries, hospitals, etc. Information such as patients' records, referrals, diagnostic results could all be integrated for a patient, unlike manual paperwork systems where the patient's details are duplicated at each location. In addition notices and forms have to be posted between the various parts of the health service. The computerising and networking of health records will also allow easier compilation of statistics.

The networking of computers in medicine also opens up the possibility of 'evidence based' medicine. Many treatments are carried out by doctors based solely upon their own experience and expertise. Evidence-based medicine is concerned with pooling together all the treatments and their outcomes carried out by doctors around the country so that the effectiveness of the different treatments becomes apparent and the best one can be easily identified and made known to all.

Consultants are able to diagnose patients' problems remotely using video conferencing thereby saving on the travelling time of the consultant or patient. A videophone card and mini camera are attached to the surgery's personal computer. The consultant instructs the local doctor in operating the camera. Pictures from the camcorder are captured by the computer and sent via the phone to a consultant. The scope for remote monitoring and diagnosis in medicine is largely limited only by costs rather than technology. For example a system that allows the remote on-line viewing of ultrasound scans together with the associated video conferencing facilities requires the equivalent of 30 high speed digital telephone lines. However, such systems allow a patient to be referred to appropriate specialists without the need for all the associated logistical problems of travelling, providing reception and waiting areas, etc.

One of the areas of medical practice that is closely associated with techniques also used in industry is the computerised scanning and building up of three-dimension images. The term used in medicine for imaging aspects of the body is 'tomography'.

Tomography is the technique of using X-rays or ultrasound waves to produce a sharp image of tissues within the body at a specified depth while out of focus depths are blurred. The technique of recording 'slices' of the body with a scanner and using a computer to produce an integrated cross-sectional image is called 'computerised tomography', hence the term 'CT scan'. A scanned image can be based upon as many as 90,000 readings. The reduction of scanning times achieved with modern technology make it feasible to carry out whole-body scans. A CT scan can be used to highlight tumours, abscesses, etc. An important advantage with this approach is that it is non-invasive.

In magnetic resonance imaging (MRI) the patient is positioned in a strong magnetic field while radio frequencies are passed through the patient. Computer analysis of changes in cells creates an image of the tissues.

A further technique, known as 'positron emission tomography' (PET), is based upon measuring radioactive emissions of gamma rays from tissue after the patient has been injected with a short-lived radio-isotope. This approach is used to diagnose some types of brain damage such as cerebral palsy.

Sometimes disfiguring injuries not only require plastic surgery but also the rebuilding of bone areas with metal plates. Accurate plates can be produced by building up 3-D images from the CT scan and then using this computer-produced image to operate a computer-controlled milling machine to carve out an accurate mould for the metal plate.

The developments in sensors, actuators and software programming has led to computer-based systems helping to improve the quality of life for the disabled. In many cases the devices are designed so that the disabled person can operate a computer either by actuating the keyboard with probes or by operating switches from muscle movements to generate the appropriate key code. This allows the speech-impaired or those with impaired movement to construct their conversation and replies via word processing type software. Because the nature of disabilities vary so much from one to another the 'interface' device often has to be specially designed to suit the individual's capabilities. Those with impaired vision can be helped to read by computers by the simple process of displaying letters at the appropriate size and in a suitable font that makes it easier to discriminate between letters.

11

COMPUTERS IN
THE ARTS

Introduction

Whilst the Arts are generally regarded as creative, artistic ideas and concepts often require a lot of painstaking detail to be implemented. The increasing power and flexibility of computers have allowed some of the 'chore' to be taken away and freed the artists to concentrate on the more creative aspects of their work.

Art and science seem poles apart to many people and it might be claimed that many people in the Arts world are not, by nature, drawn to science and hence tend to be technophobic. Thus there are those who consciously avoid contact with computers and have no interest in using them. However there are many others in the Arts who see, in computers, a potential to enhance their work or even to take it into completely new areas.

It is natural that the early application of computers to drawing and animation should appear crude but the speed of modern computers and the developments in software are allowing computer generated images and their movement to appear more natural and realistic. Any development leads to the technology attempting more ambitious tasks so that the latest applications can always be criticised. Very realistic computer images can be generated, given sufficient time to build up the image on the screen, and so the direction of research now is into virtual reality images where the images have to be displayed in real time. This is working at the limits of the current technology where realism may be sacrificed for speed.

There is a great potential for the application of computers in the Arts and it is perhaps unwise to be too dismissive of current limitations. There is a lot of scope for experimentation, for example, one artist has mounted a virtual reality art show. Visitors can use polarising glasses to view three-dimensional projections of images or immerse themselves using a head set. The artist wanted visitors to get the feeling of floating through environments so linked body sensors to breathing to create the effect of scuba diving. Breathing in causes one to float upwards, breathing out causes sinking. The body position is sensed from three sensors, one on the headset and the other two at the top and bottom of the spine. In addition pressure sensors monitor the expansion and contraction of the chest.

The automatic generation of patterns by computer software has led to some unexpectedly satisfying results. The basis of the generation of these patterns (such as Mandelbrots) are aspects of mathematical theory that have only been explored in any detail because of the current ability to process a large number of repetitive calculations on a computer and display the results in colour.

Drawing packages

Drawing packages are similar to the CAD packages mentioned in chapter 9 but their emphasis is much more on the generation of free-style lines and the provision of a large variety of colouring, texturing, and distortion options.

Drawing packages allow the user to draw straight lines, and geometric shapes such as rectangles, circles and ellipses but there are also options for drawing free-style. A completely freehand 'curve' might appear very 'shaky' so drawing packages usually have an option that allows a smooth curve to be fitted through a series of specified points (a Bézier curve).

Once an image has been produced it can be edited in many ways, the thickness of the lines can be changed, the image can be moved, enlarged or contracted, rotated, or given a perspective view. Individual images can be selected and 'grouped' so that from then on all editing applies to the group as one image. A variety of colours and fill patterns can be used. The screen can be considered as being composed of several transparent layers and the images can be drawn on any of the specified layers. This allows an image on the top layer to automatically block out part of an overlapping image on a lower layer.

Many special effects are built into drawing packages. For example, the computer can generate a series of lines that gradually change from a starting shape to a defined finishing shape. This is known as blending and is illustrated in figure 11.1. The range of options in some of the more elaborate drawing packages means that the end results are completely in the hands of the artist and their creativity.

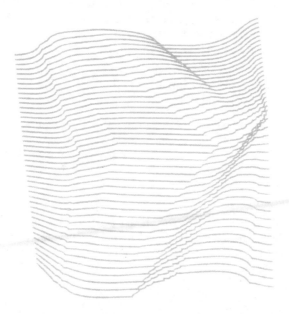

Figure 11.1 Blending using a drawing package

Photographic images

Photographic images can be scanned into a computer and manipulated by software. The software used will usually work with any bit mapped image but the options provided are mainly with photographic images in mind.

Photo imaging software will allow the image to be cropped to discard unwanted parts. The whole image can be rotated or flipped. Having edited the picture to the required proportions and orientation, photo imaging software will allow control over the colours. Simple corrections to the picture can be made such as adjusting the contrast or the brightness and the colour balance. These options allow the user to manipulate the original image to obtain the most realistic picture.

The software also allows special effects to be introduced. The range of special effects depends upon the software being used but would typically allow the picture to be posterised or colours to be converted at random. Another effect might be to make the picture appear embossed. By creating a monotone image with a high contrast the picture takes on the appearance of a hand-drawn sketch.

The software should also provide a range of conversion formats that allow the image to be read directly by other software or cut and pasted via the windows clipboard into word processors.

Because many people have computers but not the equipment to accurately scan original photographs the photographic processors also offer a service of transferring the photographic images from film to CD ROM. The typical photo CD can store up to 100 images from 35 mm film. A professional photo CD is also available which allows film images from different formats to be stored on the same CD.

In practice a user might take the photo CD back to the processor several times to have further films added. The photo CD is therefore referred to as a multi-session CD and needs to be read by a CD drive having multi-session capability.

Ideally, the most convenient way to obtain a digital image for manipulation would be to capture the image directly in digital form and bypass the need to scan in a conventional film image. A simple way of achieving this is to use a video camera to obtain directly a video tape image and then to use a video capture card to grab the image for further processing. However a more direct way is to use a digital camera which stores the image in the camera's own memory. This image can then be downloaded, when required, to a computer through a serial cable.

Digital cameras are usually based on a charge coupled device (CCD). The CCD is placed at the point of focus in the camera (see also chapter 10). In the case of colour digital cameras the CCD consists of an array of light sensitive cells receptive to red, green and blue light. A digital camera having 1 MB of memory might allow 40 pictures to be stored at the camera's default quality, 10 at its fine quality or 5 at its highest quality. Some cameras have PCMCIA slots allowing up to 16 MB of extra memory to be added.

The software associated with video capture cards allow you to set up the link with the video recorder and align the picture. Depending on the software, it is also possible to capture the sound from the video. Having connected the video machine to the video card via a suitable cable the correct video standard (NTSC or PAL) has to be set in the software setup routine, together with details of polarity. Some cards and software allows several videos to be connected and so these connections also need to be configured. The size and the alignment of the display on the monitor can also be controlled.

With the video running, a single frame can be captured by activating the freeze button on a menu at the appropriate moment. Alternatively a short video sequence can be captured. Each frame from the video is stored in adjacent portions of the storage media and quickly uses up hard disk space. The amount of storage space needed can be reduced by only capturing a small section of the whole video frame and also by using data compression techniques. However if data compression techniques are used then time is taken de-compressing on playback and the image may then appear jerky. Just a few seconds of video capture can require 10 MB of disk space.

Once the video sequence has been captured software allows it to be edited. The sequence can be 'run through' by moving a slider bar on the screen and the start point and stopping point for editing marked. The next step is to select whether the editing action is to be carried on the audio, video or both tracks of the data. Having specified what is to be edited then the appropriate editing action is selected from the menu, e.g. cut, copy, paste, undo.

Special effects in films

In addition to using computers for pure animation many films use a mixture of real actors and scenery together with computer generated images. Space adventure films were the first to use a computer-based technique known as motion control. Models of spacecraft were hung against a plain background and a film camera was glided past the model under the control of a computer. The computer controlled the speed of movement and the tilting of the camera giving the impression, on playback, of a spacecraft moving fast away or towards you and banking to change direction. The models were shot one at a time with the computer being programmed to follow a story board which resulted in realistic fight scenes when the frames were superimposed.

With the developments in computer technology it also became possible to produce digital effects on the computer and transfer them directly onto film without the use of models. This allowed visual changes to be programmed that could not be achieved in any other way. For example, a computer generated 'barren' planet could change into a lush green planet full of foliage. The technique of computer generated blending, as described in the previous section, could be applied to films. Instead of gradually changing from one shape to another as a line moved across a page the changes in the image are superimposed over a number of frames. The visual effect, called morphing, is that one shape changes smoothly into another.

Human-type cartoon characters need to move realistically. Motion capture systems can be used to create computer generated images that move like humans. In motion capture systems the actor wears a body suit with reflective markers at key locations, such as elbows, hands, feet, knees. The actor is bathed in infrared light and filmed by two infrared cameras. Videotapes of the film are fed into a computer to extract the motion data and the movements of the resulting stick figure are superimposed upon a 3D computerised character. Another approach analyses distortions in a pattern of fine lines projected onto a moving actor. Two cameras feed different perspectives of the actor into a computer where image analysing software creates a detailed full body surface. The resolution can be as fine as 1 mm square.

Another problem is 'superimposing' computer generated action with real filming and correctly synchronising the movements. This has led to a variety of techniques being adopted. The traditional method in filming is to use puppets or models with the puppeteers working just outside the range of the cameras, sometimes using radio controlled equipment. King Kong, for example, was only about 15 inches tall. In some scenes the 'real' action was back projected with the puppet in the foreground.

Another aspect is that actors act alongside thin air with the cartoon character superimposed later. This led to extensive post-production time while the images were integrated. It is now possible to scan images of the puppets into a computer and manipulate them in real time. The computerised image can be shown through the viewfinder of the camera on set as though it is taking part in the film. The actors can also view the scene on screens placed out of shot.

Computerised screen images of puppets can be more expressive as they are not limited by the abilities of the motors and actuators in a physical model. In practice a combination of the two is used, a model for very close work, and computer animation for mid distance and far shots.

Stage lighting

An application of computers in the theatre is to control stage lighting. The changes in lighting required during a performance can be complex and have to be carried out with split second timing.

A typical production at a theatre might involve over 70 lights of different types. Some lights might be spots, some might be movable during the performance, by hand or motorised, some might have filters that can be activated remotely. Another consideration is that lights in the front of the stage might be mounted on balconies, etc. and cannot be handled during a performance. The lighting situation is also dynamic in that, while a particular scene can be lit with a predetermined lighting pattern, the movement of spotlights, and the precise timing of the movements and fades depend upon the timing of the actors during that particular performance. Because of this real-time control of the lighting requirements cannot be completely computerised.

The precise lighting requirements are developed during rehearsals and result in a detailed lighting script called a lighting cue synopsis. This will involve experimentation with different lighting arrangements, filters, etc. and how one lighting setup will be faded and replaced by another. Once the cue synopsis has been developed some degree of automation can be achieved by a computerised control panel.

The level of lighting across a range of lights can be stored in memory so that, when activated, all the lights go to their preset level and, where applicable, the appropriate filters are positioned. A common action required during a performance is called a cross fade where some lights are dimmed while others increase in intensity. This action can be memorised together with the rate of fade, etc. and be automatically carried on playback.

A computerised control panel allows the working of several channels to be programmed independently thus one channel of lights may be faded at a different rate to a group of others. It is not necessarily simply a case of switching a light on, the warm-up time of different types of light has also to be taken into account. Control panels allow the programmed lighting sequence to be recorded to disk for repeat performances and printouts of the sequence to be obtained. A monitor on the control panel shows the state of the lights and lists the cue sheet.

Although a large part of the lighting changes can be automated via a computer it is important that there is the facility for a manual override on most controls in case a bulb blows during a performance and on the spot changes have to be made.

It can be appreciated from the above that the control of stage lighting is complex and therefore the control panels are dedicated and do not simply consist of a stand-alone PC connected to an electrical switchboard.

Lighting is often an important component of pop concerts. Some groups use computers to control the lighting. Once the concepts have been turned into lighting hardware requirements the 'scenes' are stored on a computer. The lighting boards are then played almost like musical instruments by the support crews at precisely the right moment.

Music

Although PCs with sound cards can read digitised audio signals a more sophisticated sound capability is achieved through the use of MIDI (musical instrument digital interface) files and interface.

A MIDI file instead of containing digitised audio for playing direct contains instructions for playing notes. These instructions control each note's pitch and timing and are played back through a synthesiser. The MIDI instructions can be sent over several channels allowing the synthesiser to emulate different instruments simultaneously.

The most common form of recording using MIDI is a keyboard, which usually has a built in synthesiser for playback. A PC can be connected to the keyboard via a MIDI interface. The keyboard will need an 'in' and an 'out' MIDI port and the PC a MIDI interface card. Some keyboards will also have a 'through' port to allow other devices, such as a drum machine, to be connected or 'daisy chained' (see figure 11.2). The software used on the PC is termed a MIDI sequencer and can be used to record, edit and play back MIDI files.

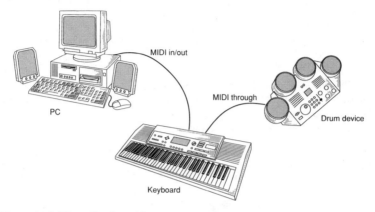

Figure 11.2 PC and keyboard link up using MIDI

If a drum machine is connected via a through port the arrangement would allow the PC to output a rhythm track to the drum machine while a melody track was played and recorded from the keyboard.

When a MIDI file is read and sent via the PC to a synthesiser each track must be assigned to a channel. The MIDI standard allows for 16 channels but the usable number depends upon how many the synthesiser can handle. The MIDI standard also defines program numbers to 128 different instruments and sounds, e.g. the violin is program number 40. The specified sounds include bird's tweets, applause, gunshots, etc. This approach allows specific instruments to be assigned by the user to specific channels so the same instruments are played regardless of which synthesiser is used.

The available PC software ranges from the basic to very sophisticated. Most allow the music to be displayed in conventional music staff format or in a simpler format for those who do not read music. Notes can be added, deleted or moved around, usually directly on screen by using the mouse. There are also on screen buttons for play, rewind, fast forward and record and a slider control for tempo (the speed of playing). A basic software package is also likely to allow the music to be transposed from one key to another.

Some software at the sophisticated end of the market are based upon expert systems design. Complete orchestral scores can be displayed as two A4 pages on the screen. If required, a zoom facility allows close-up views. The expertise of the software reacts to the user moving a note with the mouse by:

- ensuring the note ends up on an exact space or line, adding ledger lines if required;
- making the note stems point up or down as appropriate;
- moving articulation marks with the note;
- moving or stretching slurs and other lines associated with the note;
- reformatting the bars if necessary and respacing the whole score, maintaining vertical alignments.

An 'extract part' on the menu allows one part to be extracted from a score to produce pages, that when printed, can be used immediately on a player's music stand.

When played, the expert system scans for music instructions such as mf (mezzo-forte) and other standard phrases, whether they be in English, French or Italian, and interprets the playing back accordingly. The scores, as pages of music, can be saved in a standard graphics format for graphical editing, colouring notes, etc., and also for transferring into word processors.

Computer technology has also been applied to producing 'silent' instruments for musicians to practice. An electronic mute for a trombone is stuffed into the bell to silence it. A microphone inside picks up the vibrations and feeds them via an amplifier worn by the user, to headphones. The amplifier includes a digital processor that delays the sound and adds artificial vibration to create the effect of the acoustics of a large room. The system has also been applied to a silent piano. Activating a stop prevents the hammers striking the strings. Light sensors detect the speed of the hammers which control a synthesiser programmed to sound like a piano. The instruments can be connected together so the player(s) hears all the instruments. The Royal College of Music has a silent piano in its library which can be played without disturbing other 'readers'.

FURTHER READING

S C Bloch, *Spreadsheet Analysis for Engineers and Scientists*, John Wiley, 1995

British Computer Society, *Glossary of Computing Terms*, Longman, 1996

L R Carter and E Huzan, *Computer programming in BASIC*, Hodder & Stoughton, 1981

Alan Clark, *Choosing a PC*, Hodder & Stoughton, 1995

S M H Collin (ed), *Dictionary of Multimedia*, Peter Collin Publishing, 1995

Neil Fawcett, *Multimedia*, Hodder & Stoughton, 1994

R Latham, *Dictionary of Computer Graphics and Virtual Reality*, Springer-Verlag, 1995

Mac Bride, *The Internet*, Hodder & Stoughton, 1995

A J Medland and G Mullineux, *Principles of CAD*, Kogan Page, 1988

Oxford Computer Training, *Excel 5*, Hodder & Stoughton, 1995

Oxford Computer Training, *Powerpoint 4*, Hodder & Stoughton, 1995

Oxford Computer Training, *Word 6*, Hodder & Stoughton, 1995

A Tizzard, *Computer-aided Engineering*, McGraw-Hill, 1994

GLOSSARY

A/D converter   analog/digital converter; converts analog (continuous) signals, usually from sensors measuring temperature, voltage, etc., to digital (binary) signals for processing by a computer

AI   artificial intelligence; the ability to work out implied rules from a set of examples of decisions taken by experts

ASCII   American Standard Code for Information Interchange by which characters (e.g. letters, punctuation and numerals) are coded into binary

backing storage   all forms of storage that are external to the main computer store

back-up copy   the copy of a program or data on disk or tape made in case the original becomes damaged or altered accidentally

bar code   a code represented by a succession of printed bars found particularly on supermarket items; the code is 'read' optically by passing a sensing pen connected to a computer over the lines

BASIC   Beginners All-purpose Symbolic Instruction Code; a programming language

binary notation   the representation of decimal numbers using only 0s and 1s of the mathematical system known as the binary code

bit   a binary digit

byte   a group of binary digits, usually eight bits

C   a programming language

CADCAM   Computer Aided Design/Computer Aided Manufacturing

CCD   an integrated circuit consisting of an array of light-sensitive cells

CD ROM   a compact disk that can contain computer programs and/or data

character   a particular alphanumeric symbol such as a letter of the alphabet, punctuation mark or numeral

check digit   a digit introduced into a standard code, that allows the computer to test for transposition of the digits in the code whenever entered by a user

chip   an electronic circuit produced on a single piece of semiconductor based material, for example, silicon; also called a microchip, silicon chip, or integrated circuit

composite video a form of video output from a computer that combines the red, green and blue signals into one signal

CPP Critical Path Planning

D/A converter converts digital to analog signals (see also A/D converter)

database a systematic, interrelated set of data files that allows combinations of data to be selected as requested by different users

DBA Data Base Administrator

DBMS Data Base Management System

disk a backing storage device that has information stored magnetically on concentric tracks over the surfaces of the disk

e-mail a means of transmitting messages electronically

EFT Electronic Funds Transfer

expert system a computer system which stores the knowledge of experts as rules which are applied by the software

expression the name given to an algebraic or logical relationship

FAX facsimile equipment and transmission

field a sub-division of a record

file an organised set of records

file server a computer used in a network to control user access to and from large disk storage devices

floppy disk a single disk, used for storing programs and data away from the computer

graph plotter an output device that selects and uses a pen, thereby allowing continuous lines and coloured charts to be produced

hard disk a high-capacity disk unit, sealed into a case, used for storing programs and data

hardware the physical devices making up a computer system, as opposed to software

help system procedures built into software to provide messages to the user when requested

high-resolution graphics a graphics display based upon the individual pixels making up a screen area

icon a small picture displayed on a screen to indicate a computer function

image processing the conversion of optically captured images to digital form

ink-jet printer   a printer which forms the characters by electrically charging drops of ink

integrated circuit (IC)   *see* chip

integrated business system   a number of software packages linked together and used for processing a company's business applications

IPs   Information Providers; the providers of information over networks such as the Internet

IT   Information Technology

joystick   a hand-held stick that pivots at its base; the movement of the stick causes a corresponding movement in the same direction of a character on the computer screen

knowledge-based systems   *see* expert systems

laser printer   a printer that uses a beam of laser light to discharge points over the surface of an electrostatically charged drum. Toner, attracted to the drum, is then fused by heat into the paper

LCD   Liquid Crystal Display; a screen display technology used on some portable computers that is based upon polarising crystals and a reflective or backlit display

light pen   a device used for selecting items or drawing on a computer's screen

local area network (LAN)   the interconnection of several computers and associated devices within local distances, which can communicate with each other

magnetic strip   a strip of magnetic material, sometimes added to a card or label to hold encoded information

menu   a list of options displayed on a computer's screen from which the user can select the particular function required

MHz   Megahertz, a measure of frequency, the unit in which the computer's processing calculating speed is expressed

MICR   Magnetic Ink Character Recognition code; for example, printed along the bottom of cheques using ink that can be magnetised so that the coding can be read directly into a computer system

MIDI   Musical Instrument Digital Interface; a standard interface for connecting electronic instruments and computers

microprocessor   a central processing unit designed as a single chip used in microcomputers and in the control system of some industrial and domestic equipment

modem   a modulator-demodulator; a device used to convert digital signals into audio signals (modulate) before transmission over, for example, a telephone line, and to convert received audio signals into digital form (demodulate) for use by a computer system

monitor (VDU)   the computer screen display unit

mouse   a track ball device which can be moved over a desk-top to cause a cursor to move on the computer's screen in a related way

MRP   Materials Requirements Planning

OCR   Optical Character Recognition; a method used to input printed characters into a computer system by scanning them with light-sensitive heads that 'read' each character

operating system   a program used to control the functioning of a computer system

PABX   Private Automatic Branch Exchange; a digital switchboard

package   a program and associated documentation developed for a computer application

page formatting   a facility available in word processing systems for changing margins, inserting headings and footings

parallel interface port   an interface port commonly used for connecting printers to computers

password   a unique sequence of characters that needs to be entered at a keyboard before a user can gain access to a computer

PCMCIA   Personal Computer Memory Card International Association; a standard for 'credit card' size devices

peripheral   the name given to any input or output device that can be connected to a computer system

pixel   a picture element or 'dot' on a computer's screen that can be addressed in high-resolution graphics

POS   Point Of Sale terminal; a terminal used as a cash register to record sales information for transmission to a computer

printer server   a computer used to handle printing requests from users on a network

processor   an integrated circuit that processes information

program   a sequence of instructions that cause the computer to perform the necessary processing for a given application

RAM   Random Access Memory (read-addressable memory); a chip that forms part of the main memory of a computer, and that is used for holding programs and data read in from peripheral devices; the contents of RAM are lost when the power to the computer is switched off

record   a related set of data; the items of data are known as fields, and a collection of records is referred to as a file

RGB   Red-Green-Blue video signal; a coloured video display is developed from three independent signals controlling the red, green and blue colour circuits

ROM   Read Only Memory; a chip used for storing programs or data that need to be permanently incorporated into a computer; ROM retains its contents when the power to the computer is switched off

scrolling   a term used for the progressive advancement of the computer's display up/down and across the screen

secondary storage   *see* backing storage

serial port   a port commonly used for connecting some devices to computers

software   a term applied to programs used by computer hardware

spelling checker   a program used in word processing systems that checks the spelling of text against a dictionary of words held on disk

spreadsheet   a particular type of applications package that allows users to design their own worksheets directly on the screen

string   a sequence of characters, for example, letters, punctuation and numerals

systems analysis   the analysis of a proposed computer application that leads to the design of suitable software to be used with the associated hardware

TFT   Thin Film Transistor; a screen display technology that has a transistor positioned at every pixel improving the clarity and brightness of the display

touch screen   a unit which can determine the position of a finger placed against the screen

VDU   *see* monitor

verify   the term applied to the checking of data in a computer system

WAN   Wide Area Network; networks used over long distances

wand   the name given to a hand-held pen that is passed over bar-coded or magnetic-strip labels; the pen 'reads' the labels and passes the information to the computer

wild cards   used to specify unspecified characters in a field or file name

windows environment   a user-friendly computer environment based upon the concept of windows and icons

word processor   a particular type of applications package used for processing text

INDEX